MEN AND BOOKS AND CITIES

ROBERT CORTES HOLLIDAY

By ROBERT CORTES HOLLIDAY

MEN AND BOOKS AND CITIES

BROOME STREET STRAWS

WALKING-STICK PAPERS

PEEPS AT PEOPLE

BOOTH TARKINGTON

THE MEMOIR TO:
JOYCE KILMER; POEMS,
ESSAYS AND LETTERS

MEN AND BOOKS
AND CITIES

BY
ROBERT CORTES HOLLIDAY

From quiet homes and first beginning,
Out to the undiscovered ends,
There's nothing worth the wear of winning,
But laughter and the love of friends.
HILAIRE BELLOC.

38577

NEW YORK
GEORGE H. DORAN COMPANY

Copyright, 1920,
By George H. Doran Company

Printed in the United States of America

ject (except baseball, which, to my mind, ought to be abolished), and if I will walk a half-mile to talk with a man about painting, and a mile to prove him all wrong about literature, twain will I walk (in the rain) to hear him out on the subject of religion. So we fell to.

Mr. Nicholson, he declares, could tell the priests of America a thing or two about how to take advantage of the present spiritual unrest. For one thing (in his opinion), the church over here should technically be much more separated from its head at Rome, as "it is now practically an independent institution, anyway." He recited the scenario of an essay he said he would write if he ever got time on some such subject as "How Much Can Man Believe?" Quoted Newman, Matthew Arnold, and Emerson in a breath.

To-day he inscribed his check: "Love is not love which alters when it alteration finds." I observed the tall negro who attended us puckering his lips and knitting his brows as, slowly withdrawing, he earnestly endeavored to dig some meaning from this line. As he neared the cashier's desk a message of some kind from it seemed to have reached his mind, as he suddenly relaxed in a gesture of mirth, and, with a gleaming grin, slapped his thigh.

It was, indeed, a great pity—a great pity that I should not be able to stay over next week in order to see the performance of "Bubbles," advertised as "A Musical Froth Benefit of the Boys' Club," and in which Nick was to be a "black-face" and do a song turn. Rehearsing for the event now he was, every day at noon in a room he had obtained for this purpose at my hotel.

"You see that lady going there," he suddenly said; "she teaches classes in ballet dancing, and has a long waiting list. Put *that* in your book: they teach the ballet in Indianapolis—long waiting list."

* * * * * * *

Startling! Stunning! Elevator man in this hotel looks exactly like James Whitcomb Riley. "Sure," said our publicity man, "had feature story, with picture, in the papers when we got him. He never saw Riley."

Had promised to communicate with Tarkington to make an appointment to have a little visit with him. No telephone number listed. "Information" refused information. Ran into a friend of his (he must have been a very good friend, with a jealous regard for Tark's elaborately fortified seclusion) who gave me a number. "Hello! This Mr. Tarkington's house?" "Naw,

BOOTH TARKINGTON'S PORTRAIT OF MEREDITH NICHOLSON AS A "BLACK-FACE."

stockyards." Tried another number suggested to me. Got Fort Benjamin Harrison.

Admirable journal: "Annals of Medical History." Recommend it to all students of literature. Read in a recent number of it, while waiting in his office for him, several poems by Dr. McCulloch (fine one entitled "Compiègne") and an excellent article, "The Sterility of Catherine de Medici." McCulloch, when he turned up, told me he had just put Tarkington to bed with a severe attack of indigestion. Had the night before eaten some lobster or something.

Most extraordinary thing! I had been deriving considerable entertainment from the effect about me of my sensational illness. It had become the literary event of the season in the Wabash valley. I remember an English novel I one time read in which was a little boy who had never seen the sea. This situation with him had become noised about in the train as he was on his way to the coast. When the spectacle which he had never beheld came within view excitement became general. The revelation of his answer awaited with bated breath, he was asked from every side: "How do you feel now?" So with me, my inner workings day by day a subject of keen and popular attention—how did I feel now? But, I had no notion of the possibility of my starting an epidemic, of my taking it up making acute indigestion the fashion.

Yes, Hewitt declared *I* had done it. He looked wan. Had been laid up for a couple of days. Bad case of indigestion.

[52]

Easter: first thing I saw, in a front room of the Nicholson house, was an extraordinary collection of musical instruments, conspicuous among them a bass-drum, the other engines of sound unfamiliar to me off the vaudeville stage. Wouldn't that flabbergast you! I thought. If he hasn't, in addition to suddenly taking to traveling about with a professional dancing partner (about which I had been hearing much) and rehearsing to be a "nigger" minstrel, gone and become what Riley's poem calls a "little man in a tin shop!"

I was shown by the maid into a room opening onto the opposite side of the hall, and examined this apartment while I waited. Walls lined with books; large oil painting of Tark, overcoat on, crouching in a chair (in effect the work of a promising student); among the framed photographs two of Henry James, and one of a figure (that of his father, presumably) in the uniform of a Union officer of the Civil War.

There is a daughter, Chelsea-china-shepherdess type, newly turned twenty, engaged (though I heard that her father was horrified at the idea of any one being engaged before at least thirty or so), and two sons, each in the neighborhood of two-thirds grown.

Said Nick, as he finished his soup: "Now a good deal has been written about old tombstones, and the inscriptions on them, and so on; but a good and a new idea for an essay" (he is all the while throwing out to me most generously ideas for essays) "would be this: go to a costly bridge, or some other civic monument, read on the handsome bronze tablet there the names of the honorable councilmen who caused it to be erected, and then look up how many of them are now in jail."

About those feet. It may be funny that some of our recent literary visitors from London had such large feet that no shoe store over here could fit them with overshoes. But what happened to Nick? With his long, narrow feet, into a store in Boston, or Philadelphia, or some such place, to be told that they did not "cater" to "the Southern trade."

Dancing! Learned it at forty-eight. Didn't learn before because he didn't believe he could. They tried to teach him in early life by the counting method. And he never could learn anything that went one, two, three. Discovered only lately that, with the right partner, you could learn to dance by just pitching in and beginning right off to dance, without any one-two-three business at all. Highly recommends it for one subject to indigestion, as he is. And, by the way, had he told me that he had just had a bad attack? Pretty near in bed with it.

"Meredith," said Mrs. Nicholson, "you know it is Easter."

"Why, yes," said Nick; "of course I know it is."

"Wasn't it at Easter," she asked, "that you declared you were going to enter the Catholic church?"

"Well," said Nick, as though thoughtfully feeling about in his mind for the explanation, "I guess it's because I've been so busy I didn't get around to it." Then, brightening up: "I'll enter at Whitsuntide."

Well, I declare! Not Nick, after all, but the younger son it was who belonged to that layout of tom-tom in the front room. And after dinner this locally celebrated trap-drummer (as I learned he was) gave a very finished performance in all the high complexity of his art: victrola turned on, leaping from place to place, pounding with a variety of sticks on this and that, in effect all at once.

Excellent study—superstitions. What's that fellow's name? Frazer, or something like that. Wrote that enormous book, in a number of huge volumes, "The Golden Bough, a Study in Magic and Religion." Grand book! Can be read in for weeks at a stretch. You never tire of it. Full of fascinating stuff about the superstitions of all sorts of primitive peoples. Nothing, however, in the book about two dollar bills.

I had been in Indianapolis only a short while when it struck me that there were an extraordinary number of two dollar bills in circulation there. When I put across a counter, or gave a waiter a twenty dollar bill I'd get in change maybe nine twos. Because I wasn't "on," this was.

Nick (like a sensible man) won't walk under ladders; he is depressed (and rightly enough, too) if he sees the new moon in the wrong way. Indeed, his spiritual life, so to say, is rich in superstitions. And he won't, if he can help it, accept a two dollar bill. A young woman cashier (superior sort of person) looked at him pityingly just the other day, and said: *"Well,* I should think *you* would be *above* that!"

But he knows what all wise men know in Indiana, that a two dollar bill brings terribly bad luck; a truth which was discovered on the Western Circuit, and, figuratively speaking, is graven on the stone tablets of the law of all book-makers. Mr. Gates, a few days later, imparted to me the knowledge of how to take off the curse of having a two dollar bill. You tear off one corner as soon as you receive one. But I found all corners already torn off those that came to me.

No sensitivity whatever as to editions in books, has Nick. He enjoys, and values, those in the fairly comprehensive collection he has solely for, apparently, their substance, the literature that is in them. As to editions, he says, he simply likes to have a book of "handy," comfortable size. Innocent, quite, of the instinct that knows that of every book in the world there is only one edition a copy of which is right to have as one's own.

Among many other things, he reads contemporary "realism" a good deal. And he broods upon some "serious" things by his hand to come. But his heart lights up most when he beholds that sort of "imagination" which soars above the things that never were on land or sea. And, "my idea of the novelist is still pretty much the old idea of the story-teller at the bazaar." What he feels is best is, after all, "the Arabian Nights kind of thing."

CHAPTER IV

WHY SHAKESPEARE'S AUDIENCE DIDN'T WALK OUT ON HIM

THIS was the night I was to dine with Tarkington, at seven. I did some letter-writing,
and then went downstairs to look around there,
at six. And there I found him, in the billiard-
room, hard at his favorite game of sniff and
smoking one of those huge cigarettes of his
branded in large "caps" "B. T." He was got
up in a light-colored suit, with a dappled effect,
which, at least in a sitting posture, didn't fit him
very well as the coat humped a good deal in the
back between the shoulders, and buttoned in
front fell across his middle in heavy creases, like
the skin of a hippopotamus. He wore (what
I do not remember to have seen on him before)
glasses—spectacles with tortoise-shell rims to
the large round lens, and flat gold shaves (or
what the opticians, I believe, call temples) over
the ears; a heavy ring with a dark, flat stone

[59]

of ample size set in it, a gold-faced stick-pin to his tie, very blue socks, and gray spats which seemed rather large for him. He said he would be up at once. I asked him not to hurry, as it was only a little after six, and said that any time he cared to come up, he would find me contentedly occupied with reading or writing. In reply to this he exclaimed, "Fine!"

At dinner, he began the conversation by telling me that he had found a good aid to keeping mentally fit in knocking off work at about five in the afternoon and coming down to rest his mind by playing sniff for an hour and a half or so. He was working, he said, on some motion-picture scenarios, boy stories, which his contract called for in the amount of a certain number of them at a time, there referred to as a "lot." Then he fussed a good deal about the way the motion-picture people tampered with his stuff, writing into it things which they thought he would have put there if he had well enough known the game. For instance, incorporating into his story scenes in which the Penrod-like boy's dog saves from death by drowning the town banker's daughter, and so on. When he had got wind of such action on their part he had at once telegraphed the picture men to stop, he wouldn't have it. They thereupon suggested that they send on from Los Angeles a "lady writer" to help him go at the business in a professional manner.

I noticed that Tarkington ate rather rapidly. I like to eat rapidly myself, largely, I think, because I am impatient to come to the smoking and real talking part of the meal. But as Dr. McCulloch had instructed me to eat slowly, I had some difficulty in keeping my host anywhere in sight. He drinks near-beer with his meals, and when playing at sniff.

After dinner, we went into a sort of lounging-room upstairs, that is, on the same floor as the dining-room, and away from the general gathering places below. Here we were quite alone.

I told Tarkington, now for the first time in some detail, the story of my recent arrival in Indianapolis. And, in turn, he related to me, in greater detail than I had ever heard it before, an account of his own dramatic collapse, a number of years ago. He was, it appears, out for an automobile drive with his sister and nephew, when there came upon him a mysterious tightening about the heart, and he began to have much difficulty in getting his breath. He sat hooped up in a corner of the machine, and felt a decided disinclination to talk. When his nephew would exclaim, "Oh! Uncle Booth, look at that!" or, "Uncle Booth, don't you think," etc., he would mumble something which was not much of a reply. Finally, so intense grew the difficulties within him, he leaned over, and, wishing not to excite his sister, in a low voice directed his chauffeur to turn and make for home.

When he had got well across the lawn, he gave up, and fell, landing on his back close beside some shrubbery. He quite firmly believed that he was going, as the hotel people say, to "check out." Still he thought that if only he could get some sort of stimulant he might have an hour or so more. Down as he was, however, he knew that nobody would be likely to see him, and so, as he had not the breath to yell, he raised his right arm and waved it. A colored woman in the next yard caught the signal, and called to him: "You ought to tie a piece of red yarn 'bout yo' wrist." I asked him what on earth was her thought in that? He said: "I haven't the slightest idea."

He acknowledged that, as with me in somewhat similar case, he had no fear whatever of the death which he believed to be imminent, but that, curiously enough, like myself again, the turn of his thought was a raging anger. Though (he immediately added), frequently, when there was no reason to believe that he might not attain to a hale old age, he had, when reminded of the subject of the close of life by something he was reading in a book, newspaper or magazine, had a horrible dread of, as he put it, annihilation. And, too, he reminded me, we were all, when they are seriously ill, fearful of the death of those for whom we greatly care.

His anger at this terrific moment was directed entirely against one object—his small nephew. The car, it seems, had been turning about, and had stopped again before the Tarkington house. The child saw his uncle's waving arm, and reasoned, apparently, that he must be endeavoring to attract some one to him. But—in the jumble of lap-robes on the floor of the car had disappeared this small person's ball, which rummaging about himself he had not been able to find. And, as he desired it immediately, he was afraid his mother might see his uncle's gesture of distress and leave him before the ball was found.

And so, he clung to her, and cried out again and again: "Mother, you can't leave this car until I get my ball!"

Mr. Tarkington, hearing this, and perceiving the situation, stormed within: "And so I'm to be let die here on the grass all on account of a damned little ball, worth about fifteen cents!"

Found, finally; carried in, and reclined upon a couch in his library, he was there, flat out, for a week, attended by Dr. McCulloch. For about a year was scared of motor-cars, and never went any distance in one, as far as forty miles, without an apothecary shop in his pocket.

Dr. McCulloch, coming through the room on the way to his own quarters (he lives at the club): "This looks bad for literature."

Mr. Tarkington: "We've only been talking medicine." Holding out his cigarette case, especially designed to accommodate those dreadnought-caliber smokes of his: "Sit down."

But no, the doctor would not sit down; he must go in and rest up in preparation for a speaking tour to begin to-morrow. He had been reading Brand Whitlock's volumes on Belgium —"Fine book!"

He *did* take a chair, however, and the conversation fell into bonuses for ex-soldiers, taxes and politics, political events, European and international. Of the Soviet government of Russia, Tarkington declared that it was an autocracy and the least democratic government in the world. Indeed, on all of these subjects, he had an abundance of ideas, spoke copiously and with much conviction. In the course of this talk, he said, concerning something or other: "It's us that pay." That's exactly what he said: "It's us that pay"; and he said it twice.

McCulloch left us as another gentleman passing through the room paused at Tarkington's side. He had recently returned from New York, and spoke his appreciation of the opera version of "Beaucaire," then there going. Tarkington, evidently, had liked it very much. Its strongest appeal to him seemed to have been as a series of beautiful pictures, "like Rawlinson's prints," he said, "or Gainsborough paintings." I didn't myself see the Rawlinson idea, as consummate draughtsman though he was, Rawlinson was Hogarthian in his subjects, and in his manner much too burly, too, for rendering the crisp and fragrant story of Monsieur. The Gainsborough notion is an intelligent one, but (to reverse

Whistler's celebrated remark, "Why drag in Rembrandt?"), in this case, why leave our Watteau, and Fragonard?

Speaking of the stage (the gentleman had gone), Tarkington got onto the subject of plays, and associated with that, the matter of "teaching" short-story writing. He has a youthful friend or relative, who, as he put it, writes these things "marketably well." She is told by some sort of an instructor she has, that this or that story should not go as she has it; it should be "like Shakespeare—as in 'Hamlet.'"

"And these people," declared Mr. Tarkington, "who have always got Shakespeare on the brain, don't know any more about him, what he was driving at, than a goat. If he was here now they wouldn't *get* him, wouldn't see what he was up to. *Take* 'Hamlet'—why doesn't the prince kill the king? He's got him there where he wants him. 'No,' he says; 'the king is praying; he killed my father with all his sins upon him, I'll wait.' Well, why don't he kill him afterward? The king is still there, soused all the while, and around with women.

"Because Shakespeare knew his business. He's got a whole lot more up his sleeve yet, and he wants to pull it—two acts yet to go. And he knows his audience, down to the ground. No man ever knew that better. He's got to put something into their minds to make 'em think the king can't be killed right off the bat, so his audience won't walk out on him. And he frames up this praying business. Of course, later on it don't apply a bit, but he knows that having once got it over they'll continue to think of it until he is ready to turn the big trick. Oh! he was the Belasco of his time all right."

Then, the subject of our diseases popping up again for a moment, he told me the Strange Story of the Unwritten Check. He declared that either one of us could bring on another one of our seizures by overmuch thinking of the matter. The effect of the mind on the physical machinery of man was the moral which pointed the tale that follows:

Tarkington was in New York, when he got a message from Washington inviting him to luncheon with President Roosevelt the next day but one. Roosevelt had just read Tarkington's then newly published volume of political stories, "In the Arena," and wished to discuss the book with the author of it. Tarkington was suddenly panicky to discover that he had not a frock coat with him. He beat it to Brooks Brothers to get one. And there found he didn't have "on him" the money to pay for it.

He asked for a blank check; no, he asked if they had a Corn Exchange Bank check—the bank where he had his account. That is, he intended to ask for such a check, but in some way he got the thing a bit twisted, and asked for an Exchange Corn Bank check, or something like that. They could only give him an ordinary blank check. The man who presented it to him, followed him to the desk where he was to make it out, and overlooked him as he began. Tark began to feel highly uncomfortable. The idea began to go round in his head that he had balled up the name of his bank. That was why this man was observing him so closely. He suspected, this man, as Tarkington put it, there was "something phoney" about this business. Tarkington's hand began to shake with nervousness. Made several attempts to fill out a check. If the man would only go away, thought he could do it. Got worse. Said to himself, "Sure, this man thinks I'm some kind of a crook, or something." Gave up. Told the man that if he would fix up the check otherwise, he'd sign it. But when the check was given to him ready to sign, couldn't write his name, merely made wild scratches. Fled—saying, "I'll go over to my club and send you a check from there." When he got to The Players, he was right enough again. "But," with a croaking laugh, "bet that man was mighty surprised when he saw a perfectly good check come along!"

We have not yet, however, got to the real punch of the story. A year later, Tarkington was in Naples, and, as he was about to make out another check, the thought came to him, strong, "I hope I don't make an ass of myself here, the way I did that time in New York." And, by jinks, he did!

He spoke of Nick's taking to dancing, "at about the time I quit—too old." He said: *"I* was always the dancing man. Nick wouldn't." Then one night Tarkington was at a dance, but no longer dancing, at a place where he had danced for a long string of years. Slowly it came over him there was something queer about the thing. He tried to fathom the impression. The room was the same; the scene was the same; many of the people were the same. Suddenly he realized the cause of the weird effect. He saw what he had been looking at without knowing it. *Nick was dancing!* "And dancing darn well."

CHAPTER V

BOOTH TARKINGTON DISCUSSES THE COSMOS

NOW I have a theory of human life. It has been steadily growing on me for a number of years, the conviction that there is a truth in it. As I look back into my own life I cannot see that I ever did anything of my own volition. Of course, at the times when I have been confronted with two, or more, courses of action, I have always believed that, weighing the matter in my mind, I myself made a decision, based on my reason and experience. And now when such a situation arises I continue to think the same. But curiously enough, I recognize afterward that I did no such thing.

Any one (it seems to me) can act only in one way, that is, in accord with his heredity, environment, and character. When he chooses (as he thinks he does) one way rather than another, and when the decision (so to call it) is a close one, it is that there is within him something the weight of a grain or two of which turns the balance. He could not possibly have acted other than he did, as all his thoughts and actions can only be in character. I should think that any serious novelist would back me up in this idea, for having given a figure in his story heredity, environment, and character, doesn't he (the novelist), knowing his man, know beforehand exactly what he will do in any given situation?

MR. TARKINGTON (frowning): "Why, yes; of course."

MR. HILL: "And can the novelist, if he has any artistic conscience—can *you* make a fictional character do this or that, as you select, in order, say, to lead the story to some kind of an ending you fancy?"

MR. TARKINGTON (frowning harder): "Not now. I used to write stories that way. Used to get stumped, and" (broad grin) "try to think up what I'd have happen next. Now" (in deadly earnest) "I can only work from the inside out. The whole thing turns on character. And in that kind of writing about the only thing you can choose is your setting, the place where you are going to lay your story.

"You follow the lead of your characters," he

said. "They drag you on, and about the only fun you get out of the thing is the way it is done—now and then a paragraph pleases you by the way you have turned it."

He spoke of the novel he was now writing, to be called "Alice Adams," the name of the heroine, who is Alys Adams when the story opens. He "hated" it, that book, and all the people in it. And he didn't think anybody would ever read it.

"But that," I said, "is precisely what you told me about 'The Magnificent Ambersons' when you were writing it. Enough people read that."

"I know," he said, "but this is much worse. The people are such a rotten, insignificant lot, and nothing ever happens except a continual piling up of petty detail. Nobody will want it."

There's another idea of mine. The young lady of whom I have spoken tells me that we no longer say, "the older I get," but "the longer I live." Well, then, the longer I live, the more clearly do I see that my life has been all of a piece.

> Misfortunes and troubles a many have proved me;
> One or two women (God bless them) have loved me.

I don't know where I got that jingle, maybe it's Henley. And doubtless, I've got it pretty much twisted. Anyhow, I've had, in full measure, my share of that hope deferred which maketh the heart sick, and so also have I had many a black-eye given my spirit. But, I see it now as plain as print, all that has happened to me, which frequently at the time of its occurrence I thought was lamentable, has proved to have been a series of most successful contributions to the march of my years. For, more times than one, when my life has appeared to me (and to all observers) to have been quite wrecked, this has but been like (as many believe of that) death in this: it was the pains of birth into a better world.

This turns up in my mind the subject of jobs, and concerning them my theory. I hold, and I hold it strongly, that (contrary to general belief) it is well for a man (a man, that is, of good caliber) frequently to be fired. Of course, in the day of the decline of his powers, such an incident might turn out to be a very sad thing. But when health, and lust, and envy, and pride are yet strong within a man, such a happening is a jolt in an upward direction. This belief, at any rate, is the result of my observation— and experience. I thank the mysterious and beautiful stars that I have been "canned" from a number of "punk" jobs, where otherwise I might be now.

But that is not all that I think; I have yet other "thinks" coming. My life, as I said, has been all of a piece. Every part has exactly dove-tailed into the whole, like a picture puzzle rightly put together. Without this there could not have been that. And what is more, everything that has occurred to me has occurred at the time proper for the best results from it.

We frequently hear said, by persons who have waited long for it to come down heads, "Now, why couldn't this have come to me ten (or something like that) years ago?" Nay! believe you me, 'twouldn't have been so well. They would not then have been prepared to receive it to the best advantage.

In fact this (whatever it was) *couldn't* have come to them before it did. Because, if any-thing can be more clearly seen than a pike-staff on a hill, it is that our lives are the product of a preordained design, in arrangement the result of consummate art, and to wise ends which we wot not of. I waved my cigarette, for (you will admit) I had spoken remarkably well.

"Exactly the opposite," said Tarkington, knitting his brows, "of the Conrad philosophy." Deep were those great perpendicular lines in his forehead which speak of his habit of intense concentration. "Yes," he said, "it does seem that the palette is scraped, and often the scraping is harsh, always to make one a better workman.

"And, perhaps," he added, "if Conrad would look more into himself, instead of looking on at the world around him, he'd get that idea more."

I clapped my heels against the sides of the hobby-horse I had mounted, as Sterne would say, and on I galloped.

And I knew that certain things must have been laid up in store for me, before they happened, for of them I have had strange premonitions. One instance, this: one time, a young woman whom before I had never seen (nor of her had I ever heard) walked rapidly past me. I hardly saw her then, as toward her path it happened my back was partly turned. I *felt,* rather than saw her, go by, but within me somewhere I got a sort of an electric jolt. I turned quickly then to glance after her, but she had passed behind a stairway. For long, I forgot the matter, and it was only long afterward that

I remembered it—sometime after, a couple of years later, this young women had come as closely perhaps as any one could come into my life.

Then take the matter of this present trip of mine. How do you explain that? I know not how many months before I was suddenly shot, so to say, off into space, an idea had (fathered by I know not what) taken birth in my mind. Flickering at first was its life, then stronger and stronger it grew, until there no longer remained doubt that an event of consequence to me was approaching. I was only slightly mistaken in the matter of the time of its occurrence.

The idea was this: that this coming autumn (though it came in the spring) something new in my career was to happen to me for my good. I didn't know whether (as has several times happened to me before) some one was to come along and handsomely present me with a much better job. Or whether I should suddenly be moved to strike out and get one. Or what. But I reckoned up my years to my coming birthday in July; and I knew, as well as you know that you are sitting there, that a time was near at hand when whatever force it is that controls my life had decreed that I must be moving on.

[77]

A funny thing, too, this: oh! some months ago it was, that the thought began to dawn on me that it was about time for a fellow in the fading of his thirties to think about unlocking the accumulated riches of his life and to write his autobiography. I determined to begin, but the days, and the weeks, went by, and I never found the time, or in my little leisure had I the strength, to make a start upon the thing. But all the while I knew that pretty soon I should write an autobiography.

Then, on a sudden, in pops this man who owns THE BOOKMAN (along with considerable other publishing property) and says, in effect (though unless he's a clairvoyant, he couldn't have known a bit of what was in my mind), clear out now, go write your old autobiography, and don't let me see you around here for at least three months. So came to pass that which was, as my friend James Huneker puts it, on the laps of the "Gallery Gods." And if, after its fashion, this book isn't a (spiritual) autobiography, what, I'd like to know, is it?

This brings us to another thing. I am writing this book because I've *got* to, not because I particularly want to; I'd much rather (this spring weather) be loafing around and inviting my soul, or enjoying in greater number the multitude of social invitations so kindly extended to me. And the force pressing upon me which drives me to write the book, comes not from without (I could get by, doing scrappier stuff, much less in amount and easier to do), but from within. It may be a "punk" book. Whether or not it is that, indeed, is little on my mind. The point is, that I can have no peace with the world, or myself, or the devil until the durn thing's done.

So when we say that heredity and environment and all that sort of thing fixes up our affairs for us ahead of time, we do not mean that we can let up striving any the less.

"Sure," said Mr. Tarkington, nodding, "you don't just go and lie down on a sofa."

"Get up!" said I, to my hobby-horse, and on we cantered.

Now, when my most interesting young feminine friend, the Christian Scientist, promulgates the doctrine that the matter rests with us (as we have the power) to shape our environment, rather than that we must remain in the clutch of it—how am I going to get around that? 'Tis simple enough!

Why does one man born in a squalid, debased, and illiterate environment remain in it? And why does another man entered in the same sort of show drive his way out of it? Because in the one man there was implanted a mysterious something which drove him to force his way out, and in the other man (heaven alone knows why!) there wasn't.

"Decided long before they were born," agreed Mr. Tarkington.

In the matter, however, of whether your pain is in your finger or in your mind, he was somewhat inclined to think that "they" are pretty much in the right about it. For pain could only be a thing you were conscious of—a sensation.

And so the talk turned again.

It is, at any rate (to use an excellent phrase frequently employed by my excellent friend, Royal Cortissoz), a "ponderable idea." That is, *I could not,* you see, have died that April day on Illinois Street. For no man can die until his course is run, until (in other words) he has no further need of this world. There was, presumably, yet much for me to do and to learn. Nonsense! Why is a tiny baby snatched away? Why the senseless, as it seems, loss to us of such brilliant young minds as Rupert Brooke, Joyce Kilmer (my more than brother), and unnumbered others? Why does a man at the height of his powers meet, as we say, an "untimely death"? Why does another, never (as again we say) "of much account," linger on to ninety years, a score of them bedridden? Why disasters, by battle, by sea, starvation, fire and flood, to wipe out human lives to the number of the population of cities? Why does one man bear, as the term is, a "charmed life," and walk all unscathed through a boiling furnace? And why does another ("fated," as we sometimes feel) get plugged at the first shot? I hasten to assure you, I do not know.

Tarkington, who had been rather slouching forward, quickly straightened up at the words, "I do not know." Perhaps he was astonished that I admitted there was anything I could not tell him.

A number of years ago, I had the good fortune to be about a good deal with the late John H. Twachtman. I remember one time, when somebody said to him of such or such a painter, that he had never done but one good thing, and that was "by accident." "No beautiful thing," was Twachtman's reply, "was ever made by accident." Quite so! And may it not also be that no man ever, in the newspaper headline phrase, "meets death by accident"?

"That is my position exactly," said Tarkington, going back to the concluding words of my preceding paragraph, "in all this spiritism business: we don't know enough about the thing to know anything about it."

He even startled me by the extent of his reading in the more important literature of the subject, which (so well has he coördinated it) he briefly reviewed in a lump. He has seen tables moved without any explainable agency. Asserts that because you cannot explain why a table should want to cut up, it does not follow that it is inspired to do so by the dead. Has heard various kinds of "raps," coming from no source discernible to him. Regards that as evidence only that raps can come, or be made to come, in a manner mysterious to you and me. Has seen "messages" "received." I do not recall whether or not he said he had ever seen any of the filmy apparitions which are taken to be "spirits." But 'tis no matter about that.

His conclusion is simply that there is in the

world some force, or power, or what not, which
we do not now understand, and which "we are
yet a long way off from knowing anything
about." As to "communications," he made the
remark, highly interesting to me, that we should
not scoff at them because they may be, to us,
silly, foolish, and without any point—because we
cannot possibly know what a plane of intelligence exists among spirits departed from our
sort of life; if such spirits there be. Finally, he
affirmed that so far in all our contact with this
phenomena there has never been established a
case of "identity"—not one. "But," with an upward flinging gesture, "of course, if we could
find only one, it's all off—that would be
enough."

A clock struck twelve.

And so, to modernize young Franklin P.
Adams's great friend (and constant source of
copy), Pepys, in a cab with my host back again
to my lodgings.

CHAPTER VI

RILEY AND A COLORED BARBER

THE barbers in this shop (this is the following day), as is frequently the case in Indianapolis, are what is generally called "colored" men. The barber I drew was a man after my own heart, that is, he was what Carlyle, I believe it was, called a communicating animal. I told him, by way of starting the ball, that I had recently come from New York. He said that when they used to have excursion rates with stop-over privileges, he had been in the habit of spending a couple of weeks in New York every summer. He added that he didn't know whether he would care to go there now, as since the country had gone dry he probably would not have so gay a time as formerly.

He was not averse to prohibition, he said, as he thought it was rather good for him,—at any rate, it caused him to save more money. For the past five years, he told me, he had been pretty straight, but there had been a time in his life when the situation was, as he put it, "perilous." He was the kind of man, I say, that I love, for he talked (as I do) about himself, open, frank, his life an open book to any that would listen.

Shaved, he asked me if I would have a face massage. I did not feel that I stood much in need of such a thing, but I was not willing to part quickly with the society of a fellow of such golden talk as his. He explained to me the ritual of his domestic life on Sundays. He and his wife —there were, he said, only two of them—went to church in the morning. Then they came home and read the papers, or perhaps took "a nap." They usually had friends in to dinner, and afterward cranked up the Victrola. In the evening they usually started out for the "picture shows," and sometimes did three of them before again going home.

Now as I sat in the barber chair and this dark-skinned and very real gentleman attended me, I envied that estimable man. His life was wholesome and fine—and he was happy. Whereas I, God help me! as far back, nearly, as my memory can reach, I have been storm-tossed and miserable; I have found for my soul no abiding city.

[85]

There was a day (as George Moore says of himself) when my dream was painting. I came to draw with more than passable art, but always I hungered after perfection; and in this world but a very few things done by men in a generation attain to that. Then after some years, it was literature that claimed me. And I came to write, as I believe, with more than passable art. But I was possessed by an illusion. I thought that the pursuit of truth and beauty, and to seek for the accomplishment of fame, was enough; certainly it is a long and a hard, a very hard task for a man to set himself. And, indeed, there have been men, great artists among them, who have lived by these things, and, though absolute perfection has mostly ever fled before them, have died reasonably content with their achievements.

In the delectable and enduring novel by the Reverend Laurence Sterne, "Tristram Shandy, Gentleman," when the messenger arrives to announce that Bobby is dead, the fat scullion exclaims: "So am not I!" Well, as to being content with the pursuit of literature, there came a time, not so long ago, when I had to say to myself, so am not I. I had even attained to (what for years I had night and day burned to have) something of a literary reputation. I confess that in my heart this is little to me now. I am ambitious in the sense that I cannot write anything at all without doing it as well as I am able. And to be able to make anything like literature, and to read with gusto great literature, is well enough, for contact with literature at its best is, of course, capable of a vastly ennobling influence on the mind. But literature, books and writing, began to fail me. There was in this world, I came to know, something else, something more, of which my spirit had need. As time went on, great need. So it was I came to think much on religion. Perhaps I should have turned, as a frustrated child to its nurse, to the church. But what church? What could I believe? Had I— and this, it seems to me, in such matters a very necessary thing—the religious temperament? And how would I work in church harness? To these questions I have no answer yet. But in this I have faith: as the melons ripen on the vine, and fruit upon the tree, so in due session shall my soul reach its destined maturity.

In seeking for one interest which I had not, and which might be the thing which would give me the new zest in living that I needed, the most curious, and even comical, ideas occurred to me. One of these ideas, though I did not think it comical at the time, was this: I have never paid any particular attention to how I got myself up in the matter of dress, whether or not my suit was well-pressed, my shoes newly polished, and so on. I have worn the same sort of collar, and had my hair cut and parted it in the same way, for years and years, regardless of the changing fashions in these things. And whenever, at periods remote one from another, I bought a new necktie, I had been in the habit of saying to the haberdasher man: "Gim'me a tie just like the one I have on." Also I have associated more with men than with women, and the conventions of polite society have been to me of little moment.

Well, I got a great notion that a very spirited thing for me to do would be suddenly to become very fashionable. I never, I believe I can say, have done anything in my life that I did not do well. And my idea was not to become merely very respectable, mildly fashionable. I was to be a regular sensation. I was to out-fop Max Beerbohm. I regretted that I lived in America.

I wished I were a Londoner, so that I could wear a top-hat and a cutaway coat in the daytime, on weekdays at business. I would be equally perfect in the art of dress with young Wales. I brooded a good deal on this matter, and then the mood passed. I was afraid that here again another fine art would, and that perhaps soon, fail me. Indeed, I saw written on the wall, that the spirit of man could not live by art alone.

However, as in the matter of my double-barreled suitcase, I'll take no further thought as to this. For now I know that on a day appropriate to the transaction, when I shall be, it may be, going along the highway on quite another errand bent, I shall, like Paul, suddenly see in a window of my mind, that which I need to fulfill my soul's good.

But I must return to my friend, my barber. I say "my friend" not lightly, for those that one has are taken, or drift whither away; or again by some mischance or misunderstanding, the bonds are loosened or broken; and it was the wise counsel of a very wise man when Samuel Johnson cautioned us to "keep our friendships in good repair." He told me, my barber, that he had been experimenting with making "the stuff" at home now. He had produced several concoctions, not bad; but the best of all he had made, and that was very fine, was some apricot brandy. But this he kept for himself alone; he gave none of it away, for did he stand his friends a treat from his store it would become noised about, "Jim has something great up at his house, you'd better look in." No, indeed, he gave his friends "a little cake or something," but he kept his bottle for his own pleasure. A good man, and a shrewd one. I wish him well.

Then I went out from that barber shop where so much wisdom had been given me. And all the air was ringing with the gay sounds of a busy, prosperous, happy, beautiful city. The streets were filled with my own kind, people, hurrying to and fro. Motor-cars were parked in battalions everywhere. After several blocks of peering into faces, I came and stood before the office building of the Indianapolis *News,* and read, amid a throng likewise engaged, the bulletins posted in the windows there. I read the weather forecast, about what Marshal Foch was up to now, the present doings of the Marion County Grand Jury, and the latest activities of the Sinn Feiners. Then I came upon a sheet racy of the soil. It said: "Four horses and a cow burn to death and auto destroyed when barn burns in Edgemont Street to-day."

Well, I thought, being at the gentleman's front door, I'd go up and see the editor of the paper, Louis Howland (brother of Hewitt Hanson), whom I had met one time before. I diffidently asked the office boy, following my custom in the East (where it is no slight trick to break into the sanctum of the editor of a great newspaper), if he thought it would be possible for me in time to see Mr. Howland. With a large, open-hearted gesture toward the proper door, he replied: "Walk right in."

I found him, himself typing an editorial on yellow copy paper. A fine Johnsonian figure of a man, with a graying shock of hair, not too well-dressed—for which (among other things) I greatly liked him. I was further attracted to him when I found that he belonged to the brotherhood: had died several times from acute indigestion. A memorable figure, type in the tradition of our line of great editors, and esteemed in his profession, I believe, as one of the best editorial writers in the country.

While I was in the shop, why not look in at

what those there call the Idle Ward and see my
old friend "Bill" Herschell? Whose name, when
printed, but never otherwise, is William. A
journalist-poet of city life and homely things,
and far from a bad one. A jovial human being
somewhat on the Don Marquis order, only
louder.

He made me known to "Kin" Hubbard, a
sharer of these quarters, who seventeen years
ago, created "Abe Martin," and has kept him
going strong ever since. And here I got quite
a shock. I suppose I had fancied there would be
something at least a shade homespun in himself
in the originator of the Brown County philoso-
pher with the bark on. The immaculate gentleman with the aristocratic face, whom I met, took
from his upper waistcoat pocket a pair of these
fly-open kind of shell-rimmed glasses, and ad-
justing them to his patrician nose, conversed
with a sort of quiet, old-world dignity. In the
open air, and in theater lobbies, he carries, according to Herschell, a "blonde" cane.

* * * * * * *

The presence of Riley is still strong in the
community of his friends and neighbors. Tarkington, Hewitt Howland, and numerous others,

frequently interlard their talk with such remarks
as, "as Riley would have put it," or "as Riley
used to say."

"Speaking of 'out-fopping' Beerbohm," remarked Dr. McCulloch, as he reclined on a
couch in an inner office, "reminds me: It was
many years ago. Riley took it into his head
to out-fop Amos—Amos Walker, one of his
early managers. He quarreled with him later,
as he did with all his managers. Well, Amos
was the most perfect ever seen: spats in season,
tail coat, neatly striped gray trousers, ornamen-
tal vest, with little vines on trellises climbing up,
beautiful tie, stick-pin with a bird's claw clasp-
ing a stone.

"Amos used to go around to the old Marion
Club, forerunner here of the present University
Club. There one day he saw for the first time
some of the old boys playing dominoes. He
stood for quite a while behind one of them."

(Amos, it appeared, stuttered in his speech.
I cannot undertake to render Dr. McCulloch's
inimitable imitation of the stutter.)

"Finally Amos said: 'Might I ask what the
game is you're playing?'

"The player before him turned his eyes slowly upward: 'Dominoes,' he uttered.

" 'New game?' inquired Amos.

" 'Oh! no,' replied the player, 'very old game; must be fifty, a hundred years, maybe centuries old.'

" 'Well,' said Amos, 'when I was a young man I joined the army, not so much perhaps from patriotism, as because of a love of excitement. But,' he added, 'that was before I had ever seen this game played.'

"When Amos died," continued McCulloch, "several mutual friends went to Riley and said to him: 'Now this quarrel between you and Amos has been a cause of deep distress to a great many of us—to your friends and to Amos's friends. But now that Amos is gone it should be all over, forgotten. Why don't you go see Amos's widow, and make peace with her?'

"Silence for a good while. Then Riley said he would. So he went to Amos's house, up the path, and knocked. Amos's widow opened the door, and, when she saw her husband's old enemy, gave a backward start.

"Riley bowed low, and taking from his button-hole a flower, one such as he always wore, with out-stretched arm presented it to her, turned, and in silence walked away."

* * * * * * *

At the Club I was winding up the last of my correspondence from Indianapolis. Tarkington entered the room, and when he saw me, dropped on a seat nearby. "Somebody it was," he said, "I can't remember who he was, who said something like, *all nature* works for the good of a few great men." Whether he was ironical, or humorous, or serious, I cannot say—there was nothing in his face to show.

* * * * * * *

It is, as doubtless you know, bad luck to leave a city without dining at your last dinner there with a beautiful woman. And that, of course, explains my misadventure. I had, indeed, taken the precaution to arrange for such a dinner, but, at the last moment, the lady failed me.

I wound my watch the night before my departure very thoroughly. So thoroughly indeed did I wind it, that (though I had not noticed this in the morning when I arose) when, at about the time I felt I should be returning to my hotel to pack my bag, I looked at it, the thousand-times-confounded thing had ceased to go.

It was dramatic! A taxi whirl to my hotel. "What time do you go, Sir?" said the bell-boy, as we flung everything handy into my bag. "Twelve two," I sputtered; "strap it!"

"It's nearly that now, Sir," said the boy; "I don't think you can make it."

Make it? Dramatic? It was tragic!

You see, it was like this: I was not this time to ride (like Routledge) alone. No: I was to have the society, for something like seven hours, of an exceedingly good-looking and highly-intelligent young woman. "The train," I declared, "will be a moment late. It *has* to be. Shoot!"

"Three seconds ago," said the gateman; "next train for St. Louis a quarter to midnight."

Well (it took me several hours to come to the philosophic conclusion) perhaps it was better so. One can't tell what havoc might not be wrought in the mind by the society, for seven hours at a stretch, of such a young woman.

CHAPTER VII

BOYHOOD OF THE HERO

NOW, it is always well in documents of this nature to sprinkle round a fair amount of sex appeal. I should not undertake to defy so cardinal a principle of success in literature as that. And so, this chapter will contain (please be patient: I mean in its proper place in the narrative) The Strange Story of the Gentleman Who Lost his Shoes for the Sake of a Woman.

I love a ship. But I hate a train. And, though I hate a number of (evil) things in this world, I cannot at the moment put my finger, so to say, on any one thing which I hate more than I do traveling on a train at night. Naturally, when you do not like a thing, neither does it like you. I had a miserable time on that despicable midnight train from Indianapolis to St. Louis. No sleep, not any to speak of—real sleep. Decidedly uncomfortable, wretched state of mind.

Now, in this world for a number of years I

have observed a very curious thing, and one which, so far as at the present instant I recall, has not been commented upon by any one else. And that thing is this: When what are commonly called adverse circumstances have most insistently pressed upon me, and when my situation has been such that, logically, I should say, my mind should have been dulled and rendered barren by unhappiness, at such time (and with me such periods have been many) has my mind most readily turned in on those peculiar qualities of the mind which, after all, render a man quite independent of the chances of outward fortune. So again, on this distressing night, at length did the world about me drop from my consciousness, and my thoughts become filled with glow and color.

Those thoughts I will tell you—at the time when I get around to them. For when a man sits down to write such a book as this he is not, to mix the metaphor, continually to keep his eye on the ball, to be over-hot after getting forwarder with the tale. One spark strikes out another; there is altogether much to be said, about a variety of things; and if a man has a notion for all the while keeping track of the idea he starts out with—well, he had much better write articles for the papers, or things to go into magazines, or a novel, or something like that.

Speaking of happiness, or what is commonly meant by the word *happiness;* wasn't I? Very well. As I have just shown you, the idea that happiness "gets you" anything of actual value to you is a fallacy. I could still further prove this fact by a brief, five-hour survey of the world's history. Hardly worth the bother to do that. Anyhow, all the proof you need of this, are the following statements: when you are happy, usually you do not realize that you are happy. Dr. Johnson, who had a considerable flair for commenting upon life, declared that "no man was ever completely happy except when he was drunk." And, third, when you are (as you suppose) dreadfully unhappy, much later on when, through the rosy haze of distance, you reflect back upon this time, it always seems a very happy one, and exists as a valuable memory.

What I was going to say, however, was that on that train my life of long ago (in the happy way it has) unrolled to me in pictures which had been far from my thoughts for many years.

Back in the tender spring of my life, I was

fond of reading, immensely so. In those days I liked the stuff with a strong kick in it—and would willingly take no other kind of literature. And there was plenty of that sort of thing going then; at any rate, the particular kind of punch this sort of fiction had satisfied me then. I got out of the public library all the Jack Hazard series there, one fast following in my hands upon another; I went through in rapid succession all the books of one J. T. Trowbridge; and the complete works of divers other authors celebrated in their fashion.

These stories would do; they had their point of merit, I thought. But they were not all to the mustard. There was a kind of intellectual strong drink for strong men which was to be had, at ten cents a throw, in the place of "Billy" Berterman—as he was famed the world over (our world, I mean). For the adult trade Billy delivered newspapers in a hand-barrow from his store on Massachusetts Avenue. Indeed, all things to all men, Bill. In the interests of that portion of his clientele which was not quite juvenile nor yet quite adult he carried a local, pornographic weekly called, if I correctly remember the name, *The People,* now, happily (in the course of the moral progress of American society) become defunct.

Well, a little matter of twenty-five years (or something like that) had been torn off the calendar. And (so works his antics that celebrated humorist, Time) stood before Billy's window (shrunken in effect and shabby now almost beyond recognition) a human being—quite a different human being, true indeed, but bearing quite the same name as one who had stood there so oft before. And, hung from a wire in that window, was a fly-specked, paper-covered story book. It bore the title, "Young Wild West and the Mine Girl, or the Secret Band of Silver Shaft." On its face was what I suppose to-day I might call a frontispiece—at any rate, an illustration, and one done in exactly the same style, presenting almost the same scene, and in execution as innocent of anything like art, as those so familiar to me in the early ages of the world, my world.

I remember when, and with what intense eagerness, I read Mr. Hornung's stories about the celebrated Mr. Raffles. There was a gentleman there, in those stories, familiarly called "Bunny." Sort of a Doctor Watson, as I recall him—the stories themselves have almost quite gone from my mind. And when anything occurred which vividly reminded him of days agone, Raffles would exclaim: "It takes me back, Bunny; it takes me back!"

So with Billy's dilapidated window. It is— for an instant to digress—a book little read, I believe; but it is one of Thackeray's very best: that early, exceedingly picaresque novel of dashing, pounding energy, in which the flashing gentleman who plays the title-rôle, Barry Lyndon, in one of his occasional moments of reflection exclaimed: "We never altogether forget anything that has happened in our lives!" No! Back to me in a flood of light those scenes so long buried deep under how many layers of my memory! In effect, I sat (in this darkened, rolling, upper berth) as before a comic stage and viewed the drama I played so seriously as a small boy. "God help thee! How art thou changed, Elia!"

And yet, I don't know! *Does* one ever change? On the whole, I am much inclined to think not. Not all the years can make a silk purse out of a sow's ear. And a diamond, a decade rolled in mud, is a diamond still. Well, as to that, "Take it or leave it." It is not my business to instruct you, or any one. There is only one thing in this world I know anything about: That is myself; and I can only tell my story. This, I am persuaded, has the merits (whatever these things are worth) of candor as to the author of these pages and of truth in his meager impressions of the world. By the way, however, many a well-established work of literary art is built (is it not?) upon no more.

But where did I leave off? Oh, yes! The boy, doubtless enough, is father to the man. The boy we have in our eye, so to say, what was he up to? Had I the remarkable gift of Mr. Tarkington for depicting man in his natural state, that is, before the inhibitions of mature society have (somewhat) cloaked him (for better or for worse?), had I that gift—Alackaday! I wot not but this my tale would stall right here; and we'd never get (in this volume) to the strange, brilliant, and beautiful happenings which I feel now to be awaiting me in San Francisco.

For, though Penrod's orbit swung round much the same group of "alleys," "back yards," "stables," "grade schools," and so on, as that of the small heathen of my picture on that swaying train, Penrod—*Penrod!*—what did *he* know of the underworld, of dark ways and of dreadful deeds!

I should be getting this narrative on to, at least, as far as Chicago, as I have a premonition that in Chicago I shall experience divers things which will surprise you beyond measure. (But, you see, you challenged me in this fray with that little Lord Fauntleroy, Penrod, and I "gotta" stop right here until the matter is settled one way or another.)

In my picture was that (locally) far-famed organization known as the B. B. B., the terror everywhere (in the neighborhood) of all righteous-doers. To the initiated, to those of the faith, those, so to say, stamped with the holy seal, those dread and cryptic symbols rang out like shots the name—Bad Boys' Brigade. (I, like Benvenuto Cellini, have no squeamishness about what it is becoming in a strong man to speak of himself. The Founder, and the President, of this terrible association, was none other than Murray Hill.)

What were its rites, its tenets, and its crimes? To revel in those things which were forbidden by those in power. To spit upon the meek. To scoff at beauty and justice. And continually to plunder and lay waste property of those who had accumulated in abundance. (A thought occurs to me. Yes, a thought! As I reflect back upon the ideas of this enterprising organization I perceive that, though its aspirations were not, consciously, political, it was in thought and feeling years in advance of its day. One and identical was it in ambition with the forces which from one quarter so lately sought, and in so many places is even now seeking, to revolutionize the world.)

Murray Hill maintained his prestige in the circle he had gathered about him by his prowess. He alone among his comrades could gulp down a glass of water without removing a "chew" of tobacco from his mouth. He beyond all other was erudite in Billy's stock of fiction. He it was who stood, in the night, on the city's outskirts, an unloaded twenty-two caliber revolver in trembling hand, covering against assault by police the getaway of his comrades with bundles of lathes stolen from the lumber yard. Lathes stolen to fence the cracks in the "woodshed" from the giving out of light from within—where in the dark hours was a gambling den.

The most memorable event in the history of

the B. B. B. (somewhat painfully memorable for one of its members) was the casting of a maiden-lady aunt into a deep pit—she having entered the rendezvous of the gang in search of some such article as a grass rake, and quite innocent of the fact that a trap-door had been cut in the flooring with the express design of capturing, and holding for ransom, the poor little rich boy of the neighborhood, Freddie Minhurst.

At length the B. B. B. perished, and (as far as I know) had no successor. The Dirty Dozen, of a later date, an association of somewhat older spirits whose ambitions were spineless: playing pool (which was against the law for those under eighteen); hanging round the corner drugstore in the evening; wearing very pointed shoes (which were ultra then); and endeavoring to cultivate the mustache.

* * * * * * *

That accursed train stopped. Continued to stay stopped. Engine sounded its whistle. Again. Still stopped! Now what the deuce is the matter! I had been coming closer and closer to sleep! If there is one thing beyond all else that riles me (outside, of course, of encountering some pig-headed idea) it is this: get my nerves somewhat in accord with the horror of occupying a vile coop in a rushing night train—bang! nerves ripped to smithers—all motion ceases!

Creak, creak! Begin to go! Cheer up a bit. Stalled again!

Oh, Lord! What's the use! Think of something else!—in St. Louis I'll find her that I missed.

* * * * * * *

In that singular way in which the mind works, the thought of one woman led to thought of another, who had no relation whatever to the first. I don't know whether or not you have had the experience, which was mine in Indianapolis. Curious kind of thing, seems to me. You know, her name was Marie. Or perhaps you don't know. Anyhow, met her on the street, quite by chance. Hadn't seen her for years and years. Kissed her on the spot. Should I not? I dunno! Seemed to me a very natural sort of thing to do.

"Why, yes; of course! To-morrow? Fine!"

And so I was to dine with her! By the way, what was that gentleman's name? Begins with M or S, or B, or something like that. Give it up! Well, he was to call for me, and take me out to their house. (The name would come out somehow.)

What is that phrase of George Moore's? "The Romance of Destiny." For she was a child, and I was a child, I and my Annabel Lee—I mean, Marie. I don't know how the poem goes. Look it up. I haven't time to-day. Something about a great deal of purity in the loving of these children in a kingdom by the sea. Quite so!

Well, here was she, and here was I, and here was her husband, all sitting down to meat together. And that's all there is to the story. Unless her husband should die, or run away with a movie actress, and I should meet her crossing Hyde Park, and we should give a vicar a sovereign, and she should divorce me at Monte Carlo. Who can say? Not I!

* * * * * * *

In the meantime, I seemed to be again getting on toward St. Louis.

I knew all the while that he was there; but I never understood just how you go to see a man who lives in a postoffice. You know those great long buildings, with the endless corridors full of echoes, little windows all about, and everything.

But one day I was buying thirty cents' worth

of stamps in there; and afterward I was going along toward the end where you get out; and on a door I saw the word "Postmaster"; and I said: "I declare! if that isn't where he lives, right in there!" I didn't know then, of course, whether you could go in and see a postmaster, the way you might anybody else out in the secular world; but I confided in a young woman behind a railing my idea of attempting such an act. She said, very pleasantly, it was quite all right for me to go in. And there, 'pon my soul! he was: Robert E. Springsteen—the gentleman who, once upon a time, sold me my first pair of pants.

It was like a cinema: my grandmother (poor old lady! she is dead long ago) took me in the family "carriage" (that vehicle which was the symbol of some position in those days) to the When—that was the singular and humorous name of this clothing store. (There the now a bit elderly, prosperous, and prominent Mr. Springsteen was the young clerk.) I can see myself, plain as print, poised on the step of the carriage, about to alight. My costume—that of a male person of my age and caste—"kilts."

This first suit with short trousers, it was understood by common pact between me as party to the first part and, on the other hand, all the members of my family, was to be for Sunday use exclusively. As a handsome concession to the august occasion, an exception was made in the matter of the first day of my possession of the distinguished property.

As, that afternoon, I stood on the pavement before the gracious brick residence where I had been born, and flaunted the sartorial insignia of my manhood, it struck me that the world was singularly unalive to a matter of great moment. At length I could stand this situation no longer. And, with my hands deep in my trouser pockets, I said to the next passerby: "I have on pants!"

*　　*　　*　　*　　*　　*　　*

The strike of the switchmen, or yardmen, or whatever you call them, was on; and we came into St. Louis by leaps of an inch every half an hour.

Oh, yes; those shoes! You will recollect (as you have a retentive memory) that in my account of my departure from Indianapolis I said we (I and the bell-boy who assisted me to "pack") threw into my bag "everything handy." So (in St. Louis when I sought my slippers) I discovered we literally *had* done, more or less regardless of my property as distinct from that of the hotel.

I had transported plenty of ashtrays, but no slippers. And likewise to my "other" shoes— farewell!

CHAPTER VIII

MILTONIC ANGELS, NOT HERRICK BLOSSOMS

I DON'T know whether or not you have ever been to St. Louis. And so, I'll tell you something about the place. A few turns about the streets and you are struck by something— something odd, unusual, impressive. But you don't know what it is you are struck by. Not at once.

Then, perhaps suddenly, the scales drop from your eyes; and you see! What? Why, that the women of St. Louis—all the women of St. Louis! —are very remarkable indeed. A fine lady descending from her car, an elevator lass—'tis the same. Handsome all! Noble of stature and mien. Mettlesome! One thinks of what the old tales call a "charger." And one thinks, too, of that majestic animal whose nostrils scented the battle from afar and who said "Ha! Ha!" Not the petite type this—though I have nothing against that either. But here is sculpture, painting, poetry in a different mood. Elgin marble,

[112]

not Chelsea china; Rubens, not Watteau; Miltonic angels, not Herrick blossoms. There came into my mind, as I lit a cigarette at that busy corner of Olive and Ninth Streets, an echo of that line of Meredith's, and I tried to reconstruct the best of it. How does it go? "Great-bosomed mothers of the race," or something like that. Ah! (to speak in the rhythm of old Omar) look it up in the books. Books to me are only memories. I read them when (at twenty) I was old; now that, at thirty-five (or so), I am young, my concern is only with the moving spectacle itself. Come; let us go along Olive Street, and *there* read the story and see the show!

And if (and such, indeed, is the general effect of the scene) all the women of St. Louis are of heroic mold and beautiful countenance, so, too, is it true that they subtly know the art of distinction in dress. They dress so well, indeed, that they do not, in, the least, overdress. They know, what Whistler taught, that a portrait should stand *within* its frame. In this, I think, they have more or less the drop on Fifth Avenue.

*   *   *   *   *   *   *

When I arrived in the city they were putting on a "Forward St. Louis" movement. Some gentlemen of my acquaintance invited me to a luncheon at a meeting of the Advertising Club, where I heard, presented with much eloquence, the merits of "Municipal Advertising," "The Symphony Orchestra," "The Municipal Theater," and "The Coming Municipal Bond Issue." Then, intending that as an act of courtesy, those in charge of the affair called upon me to "speak."

I must tell you, in this my autobiography, how it was with me in the matter of that speaking business. Because I foresee, as we go on, some sport to come of the thing.

Now, the various writers who have told with much incisive humor of the agonies of small boys compelled to speak a "piece" at school have hardly touched the surface of the tortures that, in such circumstances, were mine. Come to think of it, my life from now until the end is comparatively immune from mental anguish. For (I see myself again at "Number Ten" schoolhouse, on Friday afternoon) nothing else conceivable in this world could possibly "get my goat" anywhere near "as worse" as that did.

Got little, or no, better in this matter as I grew older. In the course of time (and after several years spent in New York as an idle apprentice to the profession of painting), as a result of a humorous series of circumstances I turned up as a Student at the University of Kansas—was "rushed" (I believe that's the word) by two fraternities. Became a Sigma Alpha Epsilon "brother." Talkative enough cheek by jowl, mute was I in formal council.

There was a "man" of that "chapter" named (I think) Cockmore—a regular, rip-roaring genius at speechifying. As Mr. Whistler remarks, "I haven't heard of him since." But no matter, the point is (awaiting in terror the time when I might have to arise and say something), I used to sit in marvelment at the strange gift of this fellow creature—as marvelous to me, as inexplicable, as any shake-a-rabbit-out-of-a-top-hat kind of stuff I ever saw. He would go on and on and on. The fact that he *was* on his feet, and being listened to by a throng, *gave* him something to say. Gave him power, dramatic force, and eloquence, literary style—which at other times he did not possess.

Whereas with me, an organism in all its physical parts like himself, such a situation worked in exactly the opposite way. Whenever there

[115]

was anything to be said by me, my instinct has ever been to get off in a corner somewhere and write it out; if I could do that, I felt the thing I had to say would come out all right. And, by the way, Cockmore, on the other hand, couldn't write worth beans.

But whenever I had to stand up before a lot of people my brain seemed to fall down somehow somewhere behind my ears. Any nimbleness of mind which I might other times possess departed completely. Nothing whatever resembling a thought or an idea remained with me. Painfully and laboriously I would lift one heavy sentence after another, becoming more and more bewildered all the while by my acute consciousness of my singular impotence in the matter of expression. Though later, of course, I had an abundance of what the politicians call "cabwit" —that is, the brilliant things which occur to you on the way home.

There doesn't seem to be any word for the case, such as tone deaf, and color blind, but same sort of thing, this, I concluded—something left out of the machine: I was organically disqualified from speaking.

At Indianapolis, it was, the miracle happened.

[116]

MILTONIC ANGELS

Got roped into attending a meeting of the Writers' Club, held in a side room of the very handsome new Public Library building there. Knew I'd be called on to "say something." Nevertheless, went gladly. What do you think of that! Believe you me, I didn't know what to think of it myself.

Gentleman, professor of that subject at Indiana University, gave address on "Journalism." Spoke well—and at considerable length. Here comes the funny stuff. How—at all those occasions throughout my life when I would be, as the barbers say, "next"—had I yearned (with deep and frantic yearning) for him that "preceded" me to continue talking on and on forever!

Account for the phenomenon however you can: I became decidedly annoyed by this gentleman— was he going to talk all night, give *me* no chance at all?

It was a weird sensation—to see (for the first time in my life) a large bunch of eager faces fixed upon me and all alight with approving smiles. I talked, I realized then as well as afterward, too rapidly; and I came too abruptly to an end. But as I glanced at the very slight memorandum I had made during the professor's discourse, the stuff just tumbled out, and then suddenly that seemed to be all I had in stock.

A mysterious, a miraculous good luck attended me. I told, among other things, the story of the gentleman in Philadelphia. He went into John Wanamaker's bookstore there, this gentleman, and bought a copy of a recently published volume of mine to read, as he stated, on his commutation train going home. He took the next train back to Philadelphia, where at John Wanamaker's he demanded his money back. Mr. Wanamaker, or some one speaking for him, refused to comply with this demand, on the ground that the gentleman had had time to read the book. And this the gentleman declared he certainly had done. Proclaimed it, he did, the *rottenest* book he ever had read.

Failing of any satisfaction at the bookshop, he sat him down and wrote to my publishers. In this lengthy, able, and very spirited communication he asserted that the mind that had conceived that book was not equal even to the mind of a child, and he advanced the judgment that any publishing house which would put forth such a thing, and sting a man a sum of money for it, was no better than, in his phrase, a "gang of crooks."

Well, I was advised by one having my interest in mind that I should not tell this story, as it might give my books a black eye. But next morning—I had been hilariously asked, at the conclusion of my talk, the name of the Philadelphian's purchase—I found in W. K. Stewart's bookstore three persons who had heard me, asking for copies of that volume. It may have been, of course, that they were merely curious to see how bad a book really could be. But they cast my way, as I went by, a look as though they were genuinely pleased to see me. And so it was, thus encouraged by my phenomenal stroke of public articulation, that after all these years of quite contrary sentiment in the matter, was born in me the ambition to become a brilliant "platform" speaker. And I resolved to cultivate this art on my travels. Indeed, right keen was I to speak again somewhere else without delay.

* * * * * * *

But, let me see, I am now in St. Louis, am I not? A new bookstore is being opened here. That is largely what I came about. To take a part, at the kind invitation of the management, in what the announcements term "authors' week." That and to seek to make the acquaintance of the gentleman advertised to act as "master of ceremonies," William Marion Reedy.

He arose, Mr. Reedy, to "introduce" the first speaker. A Chestertonian figure of a man. A pear-shaped countenance (enormous at the base) mounted on a pear-shaped torso. Face aglow like a ruddy lantern. Solemn in effect, very solemn. Put the tips of his fingers together before him, like a Dickensian minister about to pronounce a benediction. Suggested, a great deal, a very large owl.

Or rather, perhaps (after he had begun to speak), an immense, very owlish, fat boy speaking a "piece" at school. He uttered, standing perfectly still, looking all the while straight into the air before him, with a completely expressionless countenance—and (as it seemed) painfully, in a dull monotone—a series of exceedingly humorous remarks. Then solemnly sat down. And continued to present an utterly empty face to the air.

I do not know when I had seen a character which so greatly took my fancy. Perhaps it was when, at the gate to Overroads, I last saw the illustrious G. K. C. himself.

I was told that in order to find Mr. Reedy "in" it would be necessary for me to call at his office in the forenoon, as at this season of the year it was his habit to go to the ball game after lunch.

*   *   *   *   *   *   *

My soul was cheered first pop out of the box in St. Louis by the sight of a splendid Airedale riding by in a luxurious car. I had not seen such a happy spectacle since I left New York. Much had I complained in Indianapolis of the absence from the picture of blooded dogs. "No," admitted Mr. Nicholson, "this is not a dog-town." Reluctantly, not because he himself cares a bit for dogs, or knows the least thing about them, but because it pains him to feel his city lacking in any fine quality, and he knew that I knew that a people which has no cultivated sense for bred dogs is a people by that much falling short of a full equipment of the graces of the heart and mind. I read him a lecture on this theme. Sternly, too.

Now as to the effect in values of women in the social picture, he is, I am happy to be able to testify, not insensitive. He suggested to me a

highly intelligent idea in this connection. This—
that we (he and I) propose to the editorial
mind somewhere the following brilliant journalistic enterprise: the pair of us to be sent (at a
fancy figure) from coast to coast, from the Do-
minion to the Mexican border, as connoisseurs in
this matter, as a commission of inquiry to collect
data, and as a court of judgment to render a
verdict. What matter? Why, as to where the
prettiest women in America are to be found, in
what part of the nation they abound in greatest
numbers, how the types of one locality differ
from those of another, and (if possible) to ascertain the reasons for this. And so on.

As, however, I was already launched upon my
travels, and as the business of framing up the
thing with an editor for the two of us might have
occasioned some delay, I determined to go it
alone, and (all unaided) to conduct this perilous
investigation and give you some answers to the
stirring questions I have just stated.

Rather a large order, that, I found right away.
For at once I ran up against a snag. Why (I
give it up!) do all women in St. Louis have such
jolly fine complexions? And how do you account for this fact: that every miss and matron

there goes crowned with a glorious abundance of hair?

* * * * * * *

Among the guests at my table (you see, come to think of it, I haven't yet finished that luncheon at the Advertising Club) was a gentleman introduced to several of the company as Rabbi Louis Witt, of Temple Shaare Emeth. An amiable man with an easy fund of excellent talk. He gave me (probably because I had been presented as a literary man) a lengthy account of a story he had written, "entirely without prejudice," though having its spring in a religious subject.

I do not agree with the good Rabbi in the position which he apparently assumed that to have written this story "without prejudice" was a virtue, either in religion or in art. What's the good of being a Jew at all if you are a Jew only slightly? And whereas there were divers religions, each of which was the only true one, before our modern fad for "toleration" began to sap the vitals of faith, now it is difficult to find the Truth firmly believed anywhere. Is there not, too, prejudice aplenty against Jews? And if a man smite you on the left cheek, turn to him and smite him on the right cheek also.

[123]

That, at any rate, is good Old Testament theology. Or so I see the matter.

As to art. As George Moore has eloquently elucidated the theme, only that art is best which is most racy of the soil from which it sprang. The art of a woman has merit in proportion as its qualities are feminine—George Eliot and Jane Austen. French art (to endure, and attain international fame) must be French; British art, British; American art, American; eighteenth century art, eighteenth century. A Catholic should speak (in art) the Catholic tongue; and if a Jew would make a beautiful thing, Jewish must it be in fiber. Not otherwise can there be vitality in art.

* * * * * * *

I said (I was speaking at this St. Louis luncheon) :

"Gentlemen:

"I used to be considerable of a talker. I talked brilliantly, and copiously, all up and down Broadway from Van Cortlandt Park to Bowling Green—in at every corner. Then, along about the first of July, 1919, I noticed that the springs of my talk began to dry up. Still I struggled on, doing the best I could, attempting to keep alive some sort of human contact of mind with my fellow man. But about the middle of January, 1920 (the sixteenth of the month, I think was the date) I gave up. No longer any use! The spirit of fellowship had departed. And now I never say anything at all; and when I do, it isn't worth listening to."

Speeches have fallen more flat than mine. 'Nother step taken in my new art. I was a "coming" speaker. No doubt of it!

* * * * * * *

She gave a backward start, Eleanor did, when she perceived my approach. "Oh, yes!" I said as I went to greet her, "the miss is cold because she thinks I deliberately dumped her." She looked as though she were about to retreat as I addressed her. Her manner puzzled me, too. She looked rather—well, as you might say, frightened. Why should annoyance at me, anger, cause her to be obviously so "rattled"?

When I had explained how it was I missed that train she did not relent. Somewhat more composed in manner, she became decidedly severe. I withdrew munching humble pie.

* * * * * * *

But happily, my spirit is resilient. I observed a young woman going along the street holding in her hand a book. Now whenever I discover any one with a book in public places, such as streets and parks and trains and trolley-cars, I am always curious to discover the title of it. I sometimes put myself out a good deal in order to accomplish this. Eager am I to take some one, stranger to me, in the act of reading one of my own books—covertly to watch his face or hers. A feeling, I fancy, common to many authors.

And so I speeded up my limbs of locomotion, glancing sideways at this young person as I passed on ahead of her. The title of the book she carried was "Only One Love." That would hardly be, I felt, the title of any book of mine.

CHAPTER IX

THERE is in St. Louis a lady of the name of Mrs. J. R. Clemens. Dr. Clemens, her husband, is a cousin of the late Mark Twain.

"Will you not waive ceremony," her note said, "and let us take you to luncheon on Thursday? At one P. M. we should call for you at your hotel (or wherever you might say) and motor to the Sunset Hill Club (which club I think you will find charming) and, of course, bring you back to town. We should ask two or three others to meet you."

The doctor drove me out Pershing, formerly Berlin, Avenue, and we picked up the other men of the party as we went: an attractive young man in training, as you might say, for the priesthood; and a Father Wilbur—a gentleman, I discovered, of interesting history, one-time an Episcopalian minister; of vivid personality; of considerable local reputation; and—as the author

[127]

of a sonnet sequence addressed, as I understand the matter, to Roosevelt, and published something like a couple of years ago—of much wider fame. My impression, got from that "grapevine telegraph" which is all about in the air, is that these sonnets are decidedly striking in character.

I had gone into the St. Louis Public Library (this was a bit before this afternoon) and, after wandering about through intricate subterranean corridors there, was endeavoring to find my way out. I looked, I doubt not, much bewildered. She said, the slender vision that suddenly appeared in the semi-darkness: "I'll show you the way." And, figuratively speaking, led me by the hand roundabout to a sort of trick door.

We passed out onto a stone terrace, and (I am always glad to get out of a building, any kind of a building) I was conscious of that lift I always get from fresh contact with sunshine and roving air. . . . It is a terrible thought: being at length shoveled underground for keeps!

She thanked me very prettily for a note I had put into THE BOOKMAN at the time of the death of the late Cyrus Townsend Brady. (I wished, on this terrace, I had made that obituary notice longer.) A niece she, I learned, of the writer.

(I think I'll look up some of those Brady books and read them.)

Of course I had "met" Mr. Lord. No! My! Why I certainly should! And why? Goodness! Mr. Lord was a friend of my friend Joyce Kilmer. Lectured about him, beautifully! Now. But, of course, I'd come across him. Good-by. So glad . . . And so forth.

Fragrant blossom! And, very probably, I should like well enough her Mr. Lord. I didn't, however, see much likelihood of my walking into him somewhere in the midst of St. Louis during my stay of a couple of days or so. So the matter went quickly from my mind.

Well, what do you know about that! This same Mr. Lord, it was, the young man in training for the priesthood, seated by me in Dr. Clemens's car.

*　*　*　*　*　*　*

I believe this which I am writing is what the book trade would call a "travel book." Isn't it an account of a tour? Though, I confess, the author of it does not seem to get forrader very fast. Perhaps that is because (in confidence I tell you this) he is writing an imitation (a poor one, I admit) of the jolliest travel book in all the world—Hilaire Belloc's "The Path to Rome."

I never can keep a copy of that book. The last one I had was imported for me from London by my friend Louis Hatch of the bookstore of Charles Scribner's Sons. (And, by crickety! that reminds me: I'll bet I haven't paid for that yet. It is very difficult to pay for a book which from you has gone.)

I was living in Inwood when this happened. Never heard of the place? Probably not. Well, Inwood was one time a village on the road between New York and Albany. Some of the oldest houses on Manhattan Island are still there. One in particular, the Dyckman house, now preserved for the benefit of caretakers paid by the city and as a public museum, is well worth seeing. A charming place at Broadway and 206th Street. This neighborhood, bounded by Dyckman Street on the south, Spuyten Duyvil on the north, Fordham on the east, and the Hudson River on the west, though now a region of new apartment houses with gaps of ragged rock or rolling turf here and there between, still retains in its spirit something of a village character. Its main artery of trade, what in England would be called its High Street, is 207th Street. And this thoroughfare of shining, little shops, slightly bending in its course, does somehow present (at any rate to my mind) something of the picturesque effect of an English High Street.

A "pub" is there in Inwood (or was) which bears the name, pleasantly reminiscent of an English tavern, of the Willow Tree Inn—an old willow tree standing greenly before its doors. And there to this most agreeable "pub" in Inwood did I more frequently go than I see any need of telling you.

By one of the habitués of the place I was much attracted: a gentleman of tall and aristocratic stature who wore rather lightly something like seventy summers, together with a very handsome set of side whiskers. "The Inwood Grouch" was the title he bore, and (the man was a journalist, after his fashion) the nom de plume he used for his column of snappy gossip in the neighborhood weekly newspaper, the *Inwood Times and Sun,* or something like that. Bit by bit (or should I say drink by drink?) his romance unfolded to me. He had been born in Indiana (where else would you expect him, a figure of story-book flavor and a man of letters, to have been born?). He remembered when the Gov-

[131]

ernor of Indiana had his residence in "the circle" at Indianapolis (now Monument Place), then a circular plot at the center of the town, with a high board fence all about it; and along the curb around it stood empty "express wagons" with a drowsing horse before each one. As a small boy he had run away with a circus. What more dashing thing, as a small boy, could he have done? And he had never been back since. I fancy he still had some lurking fear of a hearty parental thrashing in store for him "at home." Now his home was the Willow Tree Inn, where he lived alone save for a cat, a night prowler as wayward as himself. A black sheep and a black cat! And that's all there is to that story.

But about "The Path to Rome"? Yes, yes! That has to do with that other fellow. Little chap. Youngish. Attended evening meetings at the Willow Tree religiously. Very serious. Keen on improving his mind. Strong for "books." 'Atta boy! "Reading" maketh a full man. Went in for philosophers—Robert Ingersoll, and all that kind of thing. Well, I didn't want to take him away from the improving sort of literature, but I thought something light now and then might not hurt him. So I got him to borrow from me the ninth or tenth copy I've had in my life of "The Path to Rome."

The book, apparently, had a most singular effect, for which I could not account at all. He suddenly ceased to consort with the world of merry men. No longer heard the call of the "cocktail hour." As far as I could make out, he now appeared to go straight home from work: Probably ate his dinner there. And later in the evening might be seen wheeling a baby-cart about Isham Park, just across the way from the Willow.

Still there is merit in everything, or in nearly everything, in this world. This mysterious and even spectacular conversion to domesticity of my learned friend came in very handy—as a new topic of conversation with the Grouch. Indeed, I cannot say that this gentleman had a wealth of reminiscences. The interest of the "circle" and the circus had begun to pall, so oft repeated had I heard the tale.

And it's an extraordinary thing, but quite true, that after he ran away with the circus, life apparently yielded him nothing of interest to his mind until he met up with that black cat. Enthralling enough was the drama of that cat's night life—

for a time. But when a gentleman comes home through the window every morning, month in and month out, wrecked after a hard night, the salt (so to say) loses its savor. I got so I didn't care whether that cat ever came back again.

Then I discovered that I had brought something entirely new, deeply engrossing, into the Grouch's life. He meditated deeply The Problem of the Perambulator. He would sit lost in speculation, for half an hour at a time forgetful of the drink before him. Hard drink—in those brave days! His face would light with happy greeting, as I entered at the wicker door, in anticipation of the intellectual exercise before us.

He felt his way, finally, to a theory. His conclusion was that the unfortunate young man had been driven to seek solace in family life, as he felt he dare not face the owner of that piece of property because he had lost the book he had borrowed. This appealed to me, at any rate, as a ponderable idea.

* * * * * * *

Then broke the storm about Tristram Shandy. Tristram for some considerable time, I am sorry to have to say, had not had popular sentiment with him in the vicinity of his home. You see, for one thing, we had an apartment on the top floor—handsome view, looked out back onto a mountain. And this mountain was to me day by day as a beautiful, majestic calendar. By it I told the march of the seasons. It was noble under its heavy mantle of snow. Maidenly tender with the fresh greenness of spring. Swinburnian with fervent color in the rich glory of its summer noon. Thoughtful and wise in the stalwart maturity of its autumn. When I arose its august presence strengthened me for the coming fret of the day. At a week's end, and in the evening at the close of the clash of the city day, it spoke to my listening spirit. Spoke to me with the untroubled voice of those things which endure, like mountains, and religions, and works of perfect art. And made me feel very small and much ashamed of my puny self, because that forenoon in exasperation I had said of a highly intelligent man that he was a damn fool, and in the afternoon, him who had meant to serve my happiness had I told to go to hell. I lived with it, and I loved it, my friend, that mountain. . . . It is well to have one's New York apartment backed up against a mountain.

And around the edge of that mountain I could

catch, from my window, a glint of the ship canal, which connects the Harlem River with the Hudson, and along the edge of which, at the bottom of a great meadow, Tristram used to play. Dear me! I had almost forgotten that dog.

We lived, as I was saying, at the top of the house. And when I would be taking Tristram down in the morning for a breath in the meadow, the janitress would be scrubbing the stairs. The "janitress"—there I go again. You know, I got into a mess of trouble about that term. I *supposed* she was the janitress. That's what we used to call 'em: persons who scrubbed the stairs, and "showed" the vacant apartments (in the days when apartments sometimes were vacant), and lived down below somewhere, and all that sort of thing. But I was very shortly corrected, when one day I innocently so referred to her within her hearing. Janitress indeed! (I admit I had been very careless. Had neglected to keep tabs on the shifting colors of our social fabric.) Janitress indeed! She was the "wife of the superintendent." I apologized. The apology was not heartily accepted.

I looked over the superintendent one day a bit later. He was just arriving before his residence in his car—it being his humor at the moment to motor careless voters to the polls. And in my observation of him I picked up a number of points as to correctness in the matter of a gentleman's dress. He had three daughters, luxuriant flowers. I have (I fear) wooed divers maidens in sundry lands. One (I dimly recall), a banker's daughter, lived in Ohio. But as I tumbled to the current caste divisions of my native country, I perceived that it would be impudence indeed to cast my humble eye upon a superintendent's child.

Then, being an author, the situation ran in my mind as excellent material for fiction, or the screen. Synopsis: *ACT ONE:* Member of the (formerly) middle class—writer, editor, clubman, forebears (as far back as known) members of the learned professions—engaged in youth to banker's daughter; a lovers' quarrel—estranged; a bachelor now in early middle life: handsome, vigorous, distinguished in his calling. One day in hallway of apartment house where he dwells collides with young woman of great beauty and much fashion in attire. Enslaved!

ACT TWO: SHE (haughtily drawing back):

"But you are merely a tenant. I am the super-intendent's daughter."

His mind torn with anguish; his mad hopes shattered; he clambers to top of great rock across the street, with intention of dashing himself to death, amid the broken milk bottles on the side-walk below.

A scream! "Stop! Oh! Murray Hill! Indeed, nevertheless, I l-l-l-love you!" Clambers down from rock. Embraces. SHE: "But what will father say?"

ACT THREE: Irate parent cuts off lovely daughter without a penny. She repents of rash passion. Marries aged but wealthy street-clean-er who gives her all that money can buy.

CONCLUSION: Scene: Drawing-room in palatial home of supposed white-wing. She sighs. He starts. In quavering voice: "What is it, my dear?" She sighs again. He knows: she is thinking of her (comparatively) young and handsome lover—the poor editor and author of several successful books. It wrings his heart to see her so. Strips off his disguise and rises. SHE: "You!" HE: "Yes, little Cantaloupe" (that's her name). "I could not bear to lose you. So got a job as a street-cleaner, and in a few

[138]

short weeks saved up enough to make you mine."

CURTAIN: Hand in hand, bogus street-cleaner (in white helmet but without his false whiskers); lovely wife; superintendent, wearing top-hat and monocle.

*　　*　　*　　*　　*　　*　　*

Well, when Tristram Shandy would be coming in, his handsome feet damp with morning dew from the rolling meadow, and the superintendent's wife would be scrubbing the stairs— she would up from her knees and pull a "scene." Now it is one of the peculiarities of my temperament that I least like ladies in what you might call their scenic moments. I have unfortunately a positive aversion to hearing a scrubbing-brush banged onto a near-marble floor and—but I'll spare you the details of these horrible encounters.

On top of that was this: All the children of Inwood, it seemed to me, elected to gather in social intercourse throughout the day before the entrance to the house where I had my apartment. And young Mr. Shandy, on leaving the building in a holiday mood similar to theirs, and seeing before him numerous fellow creatures of an age corresponding to his own, naturally bounded to-

[139]

ward them, with the design of giving them
Good-day in the form of affectionate caress.

I should perhaps mention in passing that Tristram is a sheep in wolf's clothing. Honey in his
heart, hair upon his chest. Towering and fero-
cious, apparently, to the infant vision. One
small gamin to another in excited admiration at
seeing him course along the Battery: "That ain't
no *dog!* That's a *line!*"

Scattered like chaff before the storm, the children at my door! Terrible hullabaloo! All fly
screaming. One falls. Blood from its little nose.
Mothers, from every direction, rush to the scene
—fat mothers, and lean; mothers robed for public appearance, and mothers that are not, as the
call to arms has taken them. The dog! The
awful, horrible dog has killed the child!

So it was, you see, that the interest of a firm
of gentlemen following the profession of "rental
agents and insurance" became attracted to me beyond the other tenants of this building. We
struck up a correspondence. Divorcing Tristram, of course, was not a proposal that any
reasonable man could entertain.

Luckily, I readily found another apartment
not far away—down on Fifteenth Street. When

[140]

I came to pack up my books there was missing that copy of mine of "The Path to Rome." Now what was that fellow's name? And where d'spose he lived?

REWARD!

AN AFFECTIONATELY INSCRIBED
AUTHOR'S PRESENTATION COPY
OF THE CELEBRATED BOOK

"WALKING-STICK PAPERS"

OFFERED FOR RETURN OF COPY OF

"THE PATH TO ROME"
BY HILAIRE BELLOC

THE RIGHTFUL PROPERTY OF MURRAY HILL
ADDRESS: THE PLAYERS, NEW YORK CITY
NO QUESTIONS ASKED

CHAPTER X

THE EFFEMINACY OF PAJAMAS

IT is customary for a "travel book," as a bit
ago I was at the point of saying, to have at
least a few cathedrals sprinkled round in it here
and there. Just now, of course, I cannot tell
how many cathedrals I may meet in my travels,
but (we have been speeding along Pershing Avenue, you know) Dr. Clemens introduced me to
one—the cathedral in St. Louis still in the course
of construction—vast, very handsome, its architectural inspiration, I believe, the abbey at West-
minster.

At the Clemens's home, where we were to meet
the ladies of this party, we discovered that in
another car they had gone on ahead. The city
dropped away; the countryside took us. Father
Wilbur was leading the discussion of religion.
A man who would lead in anything, and never
follow. The Presbyterians (such of them as
read this book—and I hope they will be many,

[142]

for I have an aunt who is a Presbyterian), the Presbyterians may be interested to hear that:

"They have a great chance to do a roaring trade—a roaring trade!—if only they could see it. What they need is to put on, to take their book of Common Prayer and put on a high mass, less ceremonial, and in English. The people, Protestants of all kinds, are hungry for just such a thing. *A roaring* trade!"

The road, this (I was told), Grant used to travel, hauling his wood to barter in the town, and back again after a good drink obtained on the yield of the harvest. There now (shooting by) was his log cabin, guarded (thus the effect) by two iron deer (or maybe stone)—noble animals who fulfilled the double function of also holding the gate to the great park of one illustrious in history as a brewer.

FATHER WILBUR: "Belloc and Chesterton! Belloc and Chesterton have done an immense amount of harm. An immense amount of harm! With their brilliant pens, their wit and fervor, they had a very great chance. Wasted it. Worse. Threw it away."

MURRAY HILL: "Holy cat! How is all that?"

FATHER WILBUR: "With all that hilarious

pseudo-medievalism, that childish, bumptious hostility to to-day. Running amuck of everything going. Arousing antagonism to the Church among the hosts ripe to enter it."

MURRAY HILL: "Why I should have said the matter was a good deal the other way. That by their brilliant pens, their wit and fascination of literary style, they—Belloc and Chesterton—got many and many to read them (first simply as writers) who never would have read them as purely Catholic writers, and in whom thus was sown the seed of attraction toward Catholicism."

But it was no good, this friendly view: the Chester-Belloc was a fantastic animal, an ogre (where a great apostle should have been) in the "Path to Rome."

*   *   *   *   *   *   *

That watch I wound so thoroughly in Indianapolis—I had had it repaired. Was required to leave it a day and a half with the watch man. No time to go by all that while. Got the watch again. Experienced that sweet sense of a return to well-being, such as you feel when you have just got free from a bad cold which has hung on for weeks. . . . Bang! On the bathroom floor!

I can readily understand why destiny might

deem it wise, for his ultimate good, that a man be cast into jail, or be stripped of his inheritance, or suffer reverses in love; but the secret is not revealed to me why the fret of perpetual difficulties with a nine-dollar watch should shorten the life of a man—deprive those on whom he is dependent at the end, perhaps, of the charm of his society.

* * * * * * *

What's the name of those mountains out there? Ozark, or something like that. This Sunset Inn place is atop one of the foothills, as I suppose you might say, of those mountains—they rolling away blue in the distance, in that way mountains have, or at least have had ever since Japanese prints came in.

My hostess, three younger ladies, excellent— a most admirable—luncheon. I am attacked, because I told the truth, as it had not before been told, in my very penetrating paper, "The Amazing Failure of O. Henry."

Young Person on My Right: "But there *is* a great merit in his brevity. Don't you think brevity a great merit?"

Murray Hill: "I do—in O. Henry."

Subject of discussion switches to "free verse."

YOUNG LADY ACROSS THE TABLE: "Isn't a part of its kick the fact that it sounds, free verse, so like free love?"

Talk turns to "uplift." SHE AT MY RIGHT: "All about everywhere these days! One can never get away from it any more! Oh! why can't there be something just real bad in the world?"

MURRAY HILL (gallantly): "I have a number of interesting ideas as to that, but they are so low I may not tell them to any one but you." (Most chivalrous thing, I think, I ever said.)

Present a young Mrs. Booker (not quite the way her name is spelled), something of a writer, though not yet in a very professional way. Gentleman had recently remarked to her, it seems, on the beauty of St. Louis women. Tapped a tale in her mind, did her recollection of this.

She had written an article denying the high cost of living. Idea: things cost no more now, in proportion to the average income of to-day, than they used to; money has become so easy, we simply think we need more things, in particular more luxuries than we ever knew of in more wholesome times. Moral: beat it back to simpler thought.

Article was accepted by a woman's journal of which it may be you have heard. On way to cash check in payment for story, author strongly attracted to gold meshbag seen in window. Wrestles with temptation. Asceticism triumphs. Author proceeds on course. Comes to *beautiful* beauty culture parlor. Is thrown by the tempter. Pays down full amount of check for first course of treatment. Still taking it. Doesn't know how many courses by now.

FATHER WILBUR: "But what put the utterly foolish notion into your head that you needed any such thing as beauty culture?"

MURRAY HILL: "Quite so! And, anyhow, didn't I say that the first thing that hit you about St. Louis was the beauty of its women?"

CHORUS: "Where did you say this?"

MURRAY HILL: "Put the story in the mail last night."

CHORUS: "Have you a carbon copy? Produce it."

Doubted; no, denied, was my word, because no carbon had I. But I had said it, nevertheless; and I call to witness one Eleanor Kilmer Sceva. "Eleanor, your qualifications as a witness in this important case are several. First, you are very beautiful, so you have no reason to be influenced by envy of beauty in others. Again, you are the niece of one whose memory is secure unto generations, the late Joyce Kilmer; and justice and integrity are in your blood. Further, you were publicity man at George H. Doran Company at the time of my visit to St. Louis, and had held tenure of this office for some considerable while; thus is proven that you have much alertness of mind.

"Eleanor, you know that never before the spring of this year, 1920, had I been to St. Louis. You can readily ascertain in the correspondence files in your office the date of my departure from Indianapolis. Find, then, the first letter I wrote to you from St. Louis. What is its date? (This to establish the spontaneity of my impression.) What does, then, the opening paragraph of the letter say?

"Speak, woman!"

*　　*　　*　　*　　*　　*　　*

Dr. Clemens and I strolled about a floored roof and discussed politics of the hour, and the Mormons. The latter subject was suggested to his highly entertaining mind by the spectacle nearby of a row of bath houses confronting a structure

[148]

of more size and authority, all at the rim of a large swimming pool—the bath houses connotating the quarters of a family of wives and the goodly building the residence of the head of the household.

Something on the order of a handsome hunting lodge, this inn. Our party reassembled in a club-like room opening off a wide central hall ornamented with mounted trophies of sport in forest and river.

What was the status of two dollar bills in Missouri? Perfectly good money there, it seems. And the subject of superstitions led on the talk to the engrossing matter of prejudices. One would have thought, perhaps, that the world war would have knocked out, pretty much for keeps, prejudices one time very common against a couple of things which became of such universal use in it.

Not at all a long memory is required to recall the time when, to the mind of the good burgher, it was a very loathsome thing indeed for any one to smoke a cigarette. Only those nincompoop beings contemptuously called "dudes" did smoke them. Also, paradoxically enough, these despicable little rolls were supposed to be very deadly, and it was the fashion to refer to them as "coffin nails." So it was in those days. . . . Well, some-one lit a cigarette along the Rhine. And cigarettes began to glow in Flanders. Cigarettes moved out from England. Cigarettes poured across the seven seas. Cigarettes and cigarettes and cigarettes! Fortresses and cathedrals fell, ministries tumbled and dynasties were over-thrown, the while nurses and nuns became tobacconists and dispensed cigarettes beyond all range of computation.

Kind of a jolt to one, then, to discover round about the Middle West that candidates for of-fices within the gift of the people are forbidden by their groomers to smoke cigarettes while en-gaged in making a good impression in the rural districts—or to wear wrist-watches there.

MURRAY HILL: "It's curious, too, about those two prejudices, as cowboys (who certainly have never been associated with the idea of molly-coddlism) have always smoked cigarettes; and wrist-watches, long before the great vogue they attained in the recent war, were worn by officers of the old United States Army."

MR. LORD: "But the cowboys' cigarettes, and the Mexicans'. were the 'roll your own' variety."

THE EFFEMINACY OF PAJAMAS

MRS. BOOKER: "While aboard a mustang! Or busting bronco."

MURRAY HILL: "One hand on hip."

MR. LORD: "And I think it would be found that a 'tailor-made cigarette' didn't go with them, either."

The idiosyncrasies of similar prejudices then taken up: The aversion among the plain people at one time to "cuffs" on trousers. In the Middle West, till not long ago, the popular contempt for duck trousers, or "ice cream pants." And the notion until recently rather general that there was something snobbish about not wearing suspenders. Of a very pleasant prejudice new to me I heard, too; that for long the backbone, so to say, of Missouri had regarded the wearing of pajamas as effeminate, but night-shirts were masculine.

* * * * * * *

No, Mrs. Booker did not think that women in politics would "ever stand" for the spread-eagle bunkum of the usual man-made political speech. They, women, wanted (jolly phrase!) to "take something home with them."

General squabble in argument precipitated by this assertion. But Mrs. Booker had *just been*

to a women's political gathering. No bombast;
no fustian; no sob stuff; practical, sensible, talk,
to the point throughout, always something said
that you could take home with you. Well, yes;
it was fairly generally agreed that mainly it was
rather a high type of woman that was now doing
the political speaking.

* * * * * * *

"Speaking," the topic being up, there was, you
know, the matter of that speechifying in which I
was involved. And a terrible bad place to speak,
St. Louis, I heard. No rise at all to an audience
there. Notorious, this was. A saying among
actors, said Father Wilbur, that the two worst
things in the practice of their profession were St.
Louis and Holy Week.

* * * * * * *

Bounding cityward. But five of us of the party
remaining together. Much talk, turning now to
the early French aristocracy of St. Louis, then
on the Catholic world that is here, and again on
the great German population of the city. I
scented, with something of a thrill at the enduring romance of the human story, the vital part
played in social caste by races and religions here
. . . the moving forces that have woven the rich

tapestry of history. And I had the wish that my stay was to be much longer in St. Louis, that I might have unfolded before me in the fullness of its color and intricacy of its design the play of these various social elements in juxtaposition. Something of a similar situation, of course, is to be found in any spot which men inhabit in any numbers; but I got, in a quick impression, the idea that in St. Louis lines are perhaps more sharply drawn and unrelated elements more compact than is the case everywhere. Perhaps not, though I hope this is so.

* * * * * * *

Mrs. Booker had recently gone to an atheistic funeral. For her a Latin funeral!

FATHER WILBUR: "Yes, the dignity of detached objectivity. Freedom from sentimentality, there is a great need for more of it—a great need! I talked with I know not how many doughboys who told me they *yearned* for such a thing."

I had met in Indianapolis the trail of young Walpole; in St. Louis I again came upon the tracks of his recent clipping about over here. Was to be put up while in the city by some people living rather remote from the center of things.

Couldn't make it out there and back in time for his lecture the night of his arrival. So they, persons having his doings in hand, switched him for his make-up to a home nearer his stage. Now this household consisted solely of women, though of that he was in no way advised. "How, then," exclaimed Mrs. Booker, *"could* he have known, and *instantly,* what he did!"

Had lost his dress-shirt "studs." Dire predicament! Because, glancing quickly about, "You wouldn't, of course, have anything like that here."

Mrs. Booker: "Yes; but what could have told him that there was not a *father,* or a *brother,* if not a husband, about here? Oh, no; he knew it right off!"

* * * * * * *

Interesting case; Father Wilbur's Roosevelt sonnet sequence stunt. Never before had felt the impulse to write anything. "Kind of a fit," he declared, suddenly took hold of him. Worked like fury at the things until they were "finished," or rather, he added, until he was "through with them." No desire since to write. Doubted much whether he would ever have again.

CHAPTER XI

A VERY engaging thing, that, a very engaging thing, indeed: Father Wilbur's attitude toward writing. Sound, sensible, wholesome, upright, idea. Man doesn't care a rap whether he writes or not. Most of the people in the world, as well as I can make out, are unable to rid themselves of a peculiar notion that there is some reason why they should try to "write." What is it, this mysterious property possessed by "writing," this (apparently universal) magnetic quality exercised by the thing? Everybody doesn't spend his evenings studying to be an acrobat, does he? And she? And that, certainly, I confess to regarding as presenting the effect of a highly exhilarating occupation.

Have I not for years as publishers' reader and magazine editor been "fed up" with appeals from persons beyond number all apparently coveting beyond all other satisfactions in life the prospect

[155]

of getting something "published"? Have I not
in the exercise of my profession repeatedly experienced the attempts of young women of excellent standing to pull on me all sorts of sex
appeal in their endeavor to enflame in their be-
half the editorial judgment? Did I not, shortly
before the start of my present travels, receive
overtures of the following humorous circumstances? . . . A gentleman, and (I hope) a
Christian, novelist of large sales and admirable
literary reputation, poet of talent, playwright of
more than considerable success, unknown to me
personally, writes me a letter, professes for me
enormous esteem. Declares there is not known
to him by fame any one he should so much desire
to cultivate meeting. It appeared that his wife
was quite one with him in these sentiments: could
I not be available to them one evening soon, very
soon, for dinner? And, by the way, his wife had
recently become a poet, had just written a number of poems of remarkable power, acknowledged
to be this by all their friends. Having to do, in
a way, with magazine editing, perhaps I'd be interested in seeing several of these, which he enclosed. Conclusion of letter: "One poem, one
dinner." Well, I wish to insert here in this book

what might be called a "reading notice" to this effect: I accepted this proposal in good faith; took more than one of the poems; and have as yet heard nothing further concerning this dinner. Also, though that perhaps is a matter a bit beside the point, I liked the poems, actually, and more than a little.

"Starring" the country, then, as celebrated editor and author (that, naturally, was the way my press agent matter went out), comes round a lady to my hotel, in her own car, woman of means and social position. Now there is a great deal of secrecy about this thing. I am the very person she has been wanting for years to find. You see, she has a manuscript, on which she has spent a great deal of toil. (It develops that this manuscript is several thousand pages in length, typed single space and with practically no margins.) She could not bring herself to submit it to a publishing house until she had received some "friendly, expert" advice upon it. She cannot begin to tell me how *very* much she appreciates my very great kindness, given to a stranger, and busy as I am, and all that, but she *knows* I will not refuse to look it over. What she *really* wants to know is whether she is "wasting her time with her writing," or whether she "ought to persevere in it." Now I'll be *perfectly frank,* won't I?

An easy enough question, that, to answer. Take the word of H. G. Wells for it. He says somewhere (in effect) that the most remarkable thing about the writing bug is that you can't kill it with a club. Take Meredith Nicholson's word for it, as delivered across one of the tables of the very pretty and quite new little hotel of his town, the Lincoln: that no one can "teach" another the art of writing, beyond imparting a few conventions of construction, and they are dangerous things, too; that if any one really has the writing instinct he finds his way in the darkest alley, and nothing short of death can stop him from writing. Or take my word for it: that if nature has made you a writer (which, however, I regard as highly unlikely) you are wiser in your own conceit than twenty men who can render a reason why you are wasting your time.

Came another lady to my hotel. A third did press me by telephone. Several by letter. Manuscripts all had they. And the matter was urgent.

* * * * * * *

A FAREWELL FROM W. M. REEDY

I sat in the front row awaiting my turn. Nearest to me among the speakers for the day were Dr. Arthur E. Bostwick, a native of Connecticut, associated in his career as editor and librarian with various publications and libraries, editor of the Scientific Department of *The Literary Digest* since 1891, Librarian of the St. Louis Public Library since 1919, and author of several books; and Percival Chubb, born in England, twice president of the Drama League of America, and a writer of much accomplishment in the field of ethics and religion. I was at my new studies. I remember a number of years ago to have seen Albert J. Beveridge leave his chair as though it were a catapult suddenly brought into action upon him as its missile, shoot his cuffs at the audience, and split into a roar: *"This Time Fair Play Wins!"* I recall that I marveled at the electric effect of this line on his hearers. His argument did not strike me as compelling. Certainly, it *reads* simple enough.

And there, I came to see with some clearness when I entered upon a professional interest in public speaking—and there you are! A thing may read beautifully, and it won't talk, or "speak" at all. Conversely, a man (if he is skilled in the manner of doing it) can spout with very fair success, and even more than very fair success, a rigmarole which a self-respecting compositor would be ashamed to set. Did I not but the afternoon before listen in this hall to as arrant a conglomeration of inane bromidiams as ever was lifted in one lot from the "exchange columns" of newspapers?

Just to show you what is possible in this world, though I would not have believed it possible, I'll retell one of this speaker's witticisms. No, I haven't the heart to do it.

Nobody egged him, this humorist; no, he arose on his toes; smiled blandly, sublime in confidence in the security of his effect; and bowed with arrogant modesty to a hearty hand.

I got to like the fellow, rather, myself. When he had dumped his whole stock of canned goods on us, I heard a man in the rear of me exclaim: "I say, he's some whirlwind!"

* * * * * * *

The speakers to-day were not of the "whirlwind" sort. While I felt that they did not fail to command respect, I could not perceive that they were nearly so much enjoyed. Admirable, in particular (to my mind) was Dr. Bostwick, in the march of his thought. His subject: "Socializing the Library." But—an evangelist frequently is not a diplomat.

This whole show, you remember ("Author's Week," as the program entitled it), was in celebration of the opening of a new, and a large and handsome, bookstore in St. Louis. And, naturally, it was staged with the object of at once establishing a *clientele* designed as a flying start in the *business of selling books,* at this store. Our distinguished, and admirably disinterested, librarian, was thinking rather of *reading* books: that is, of the commerce of the mind, and how best *this* business should be conducted. And throughout the elaboration of his theme ran the refrain that it was not necessary to own a book physically in order to possess it with the mind, that even a few great books sufficed to educate a man, that it was not wise for one to clutter up his house with all the new books that came out, that if one had a desire to keep abreast of all that was the talk of the hour, let him come to the Library and take out these volumes, and then let him buy in the course of the year the few of them which he was assured his spirit required to abide with him. An eloquent discourse, sound in wind and limb—and applauded with enthusiasm by the large company of potential book buyers which had been so skillfully assembled there.

*   *   *   *   *   *   *

I am very eager to go out and have that interview I promised myself with William Marion Reedy.

But it really would seem that I ought first to give my own lecture, everybody being here and everything. I have got hold of at least one of the prime tricks of the trade—you long since will have perceived that I am very *naïve* in this matter. As I am in all that I write. And, indeed, that is art—the simple mind, courageous of its simplicity; the innocent eye receiving the world as though no eye had ope'd upon it before.

I had got hold of the knowledge that "lecturing," at least in one of its aspects, is much easier than writing or painting. I mean, of course, that every time you write something, an article, an essay, a poem or a book, or sculpture something, or paint something, you "gotta" go and *create* something; construct and complete something you never got away

[162]

with before, something *new,* never was in the world before, that thing, whether good or no good. But (so to say) once you have your little lecture doped out you can go on shootin' it all over the lot. "Not at all!" interrupts Dr. Richard Burton, the veteran lecturer (and professor and author), rising. "Every time you face an audience you have a *new audience.* And let me tell you, that means a new appeal is, as you would say, 'up to you.' "

"And," cries out Mr. Heckler, "what about music? Do you think because a musician plays over and over again the same composition he does not each time expend the energy of recreating the spirit of it?"

*   *   *   *   *   *   *

As I was saying, I now know what every lecturer knows: that you can kill any number of birds with one stone. And had I not a theme of indisputably universal interest?

HOW TO SUCCEED AS AN AUTHOR

So I began as I had begun before: "I am frequently asked one question. And that is, How to attain to success in literature. I suppose I am asked because I am such a successful author.

(Applause.) As last winter, you know, I published two books in one day: one in the forenoon and the other shortly after lunch. (Titters.)

"Now some people say that this is a question that cannot be answered—that no one can tell another how to become a successful writer. But that idea is a fallacy. I can tell you in six words how to attain to success in literature. (Breathless excitement throughout the house.)

"The matter is a very simple one. Though for about twenty years I lived in poverty and was kicked all over the lot because I did not know the secret. Then suddenly I found it, the key. The way to do the trick is this:

"By the exercise of sufficient political sagacity you obtain a job as an editor of a first-rate magazine and literary adviser to a flourishing publishing house—and then you accept all your own stuff. (Dismay in audience.)

"I'll take anything that I write." (Laughter and cheers.)

* * * * * * *

I don't know whether or not Catholic Fathers are not subject to traffic regulations. What I have in mind is this—or, at any rate, this is the way I am coming to it.

A FAREWELL FROM W. M. REEDY

Doubtless, you were much struck by the startling alteration in appearance, a year or so ago, of *The Queen's Work*. You will recall that formerly your copies of this magazine published by the Jesuit Fathers had that curious effect to the eye of being a Sunday school paper published sometime about the early 'forties. Suddenly revolutionized in format, it sprang forth with all the snap and modernity of *The Saturday Evening Post*. It is, you know, my friend, Reverend Edward F. Garesché, S. J., who is the editor—or, at least, who was for long, until he sailed the other day for a year's meditation in Europe.

A Borrovian literary chronicle such as this, ranging through St. Louis, a deuce of a thing 'twould be to leave out of it Father Garesché, author for a number of years of an average of four books (devotional books) a year, this year seven.

A bland young man (somewhat short of "middle life"), in whose amiable and estimable character I had, from the outset of our acquaintance, always reposed the utmost confidence (until this experience), he took me in his "tin Lizzie" (the tinniest "tin Lizzie" I ever saw!) for a spin about the city. 'Atta fierce animal, I tell you, that "Lizzie" of his! She never paused (as far as I can recollect) for three hours. She would leap into the air, and come down with the sound of a large can of nails crashing to the pavement from aloft. She switched round corners on one leg. Would point her nose toward the ground, then rear on her hind feet. It seems to me I have heard motorists talk about "the right of way"; my dear Father Garesché (if he had ever heard of the thing) apparently assumed that the Lord had given it always to him. And smiling away like a house afire, he never left off discussing the merits of religion, our common friends, and St. Louis, all the while.

* * * * * * *

Yes, I forgot; once we stopped, at St. Louis University. I think I felt it, or least something of it: its romance, its beauty; the romance of venerable, ancient tradition, the beauty of austerity. Dark, and in effect dusty, within. The long, long, black corridors—through them striding for exercise, to and fro, silently, each alone, in their cassocks, a number of the Fathers. The tiny, harsh little rooms in which they dwell! In one, a gaunt figure smoking a pipe. The remoteness from the gleaming, teeming scene at the Statler! The remoteness from the life of Murray Hill, fashionable vagabond!

* * * * * * *

With Dr. Bostwick to luncheon at the City Club, a populous and cheerful organization maintaining an upper floor in an office building downtown. Holding forth at what I heard was called the "radical table," Father Wilbur. Called on this group on our way out. Present, a gentleman whose wife, it was joyously proclaimed, was in the penitentiary. Her disagreement with the authorities something political. "Though the club as a whole really is rather conservative in flavor," said Dr. Bostwick, as we passed out.

* * * * * * *

A good deal of the time, when seated, wears his legs tucked under his bulk, in such wise as to present an entertaining resemblance to a frog. Frequently drops open his mouth, and for a moment lets it hang so, as though this enabled him the better to think.

"Well," said Mr. Reedy, with a decidedly sad expression, "I don't suppose the stuff will ever come back again, and it seems to be becoming more difficult to marry all the while."

[167]

His job, he said, "couldn't be left outside the door at night." It was too much for one man and not enough for two. Of his own stuff: "It goes well enough with a class of people who like a slightly radical flavor; who like some dress to the style, and yet don't want to see a fellow wear spats and carry a little cane." Standing very yellow in the corner, my own stick gave something of a self-conscious start, I felt.

On English writing versus American writing: "We," rather wearily, "all write for money over here—always in a hurry—no time, no time to polish up. When an Englishman gets four hundred pounds a year—enough to keep his top hat —he's satisfied.

"Timeliness, too, is our curse. Everything done over here with some journalistic point. Take the English papers, front page of the *Spectator,* no timeliness whatever. Likely to give the whole thing to a review of a reprint of Cowper." He greatly admired one of Gamaliel Bradford's recently published "Portraits of American Women." "No notion of timeliness to the thing. All writing now is propaganda," he said. This gave me a thought which had not occurred to me before. "Nearly all," I reflected, "except mine."

Conrad? For the fun of the thing, I have recently been collecting, as you might say, adverse opinions on Conrad. There seems to be rising a pronounced anti-Conrad tide. Shortly before I left New York I was much amused at hearing A. Edward Newton deliver in my office a tirade against the acclaimed supreme master. From Mr. Nicholson, on my way, I picked up this: "Conrad writes adventure stories, but he doesn't write adventure stories as adventure stories should be written." Mr. Reedy's comment: "I find him pretty tedious."

He continued his solemnly delivered, humorous lamentations. Our job, professional reading, left no time, no energy, for any *real* reading: that is for reading purely for refreshment, or for the good of one's soul. For how long a time had he wanted to re-read Boswell! Also, in this business a man got so he *couldn't* read any other way —always reading against time, in a hurried, skipping, professional way. Had he not, not long ago, after for years promising himself this pleasure, again taken up "Don Quixote"?

[169]

Found he no longer had the patience to deliver himself over to the spell of that glorious book.

Yes, one got a hardening of the intellectual arteries. He did not go anywhere much any more. The last time he was on East, and with the boys (these juvenile characters being Tom Daly, A. Edward Newton and Christopher Morley), it bored him, almost, to listen to the prattle of their enthusiasm; to feel from apart the rosy glow of youth in which they lived in a sort of fairyland of books and affairs.

"Yes; youth is the thing; that's the great, the only gift! All that stands is the voice of youth. Nobody ever produced anything after he was no longer young. Call the roll," he said, and he began . . .

"Not always," I replied, "there are exceptions."

"Name them!" he cried.

"Well," I said, "wasn't Defoe fifty, sixty, seventy, or something like that when he wrote 'Crusoe'?"

"Oh!" he exclaimed; "but he wrote of his youth; that's the only way it is done."

I don't know about that, altogether. The idea is an excellent theme for an essay; and when

A FAREWELL FROM W. M. REEDY

I return from my travels I'll turn the matter over in my mind, and see what may be made of it. Anyhow, there's a great deal of truth in what he said. And I let him have his way.

Where was my trip taking me?

Eventually, I replied, to California. Ah! he had been thinking of going out to the Democratic convention. "But," he stopped suddenly, as though arrested by a disturbing thought; "anybody found out there is liable to be nominated!" And a ringing burst of Chestertonian laughter, as (both of us bowing) I crossed his threshold, was his parting word. A noble monument, forever fixed in my mind!

CHAPTER XII

MRS. JOYCE KILMER AT WALNUT HILLS

HEARD about the murder?" He bellowed the question, this very ruddy, very fat man who was shaving.

I had been intending, so to say, to take up the Mississippi River as I was taking leave of that classic stream. But, as you see, my attention was distracted.

He had that grotesquely rotund effect presented by a fat man in an undershirt. His stocky legs (encased in loud checks) were planted far apart, his back toward us, his chubby chin lifted as far as it would go upward, as he scraped his bulky throat. His recognized (and ardent) auditor, a lanky negro (with a very pimply face) seated in the washroom smoking a pipe.

"That's what she says, 'Heard about the murder?' 'In Dallas?' I says. 'In Dallas, hell!' Nell says; 'right there on that bed what you slept in last night!' She pulled back a piece of carpet and there on that new pine floor they had there, was a great big spot of blood. Then she turned down the sheets and there was a bran' new mattress—I guess the other one hadda been soaked."

"Didn't it make you nervous, havin' jess slep' in that bed?" inquired the negro; eyeing the fat man with something like pride in being in such close proximity to one who had recently had such an awful experience.

The fat man lowered his razor, turned and faced the other, looking at him with pop eyes. Then he burst into an enormous guffaw: "I didn't stay there no more nights!" He returned to his shaving apparently hugely amused at his recollection of the fright he had got.

The circumstances of this crime as they had been presented in the local papers were discussed. "Yes," remarked the fat man, "it's the wimmin do all the shootin' in Texas."

*   *   *   *   *   *   *

The newsman entered the compartment with a pile of magazines. "Do you read?" he asked. I shook my head, "No."

*   *   *   *   *   *   *

I was back-tracking to Cincinnati, having an appointment there which could not be made at any other time. I was much struck by the sky.

[173]

The idea occurred to me that one of the spiritual and esthetic advantages of riding on trains is the excellent opportunity this gives you for contemplating and reflecting upon the sky. Not

> Upon that little tent of blue
> Which prisoners call the sky.

A vast thing! Full (on a day like this) of rich argosies, great chariots, and noble chargers. Now, it is a curious thing, when I look at the sea I realize what a tiny atom I am; and I feel very small indeed inside; but when I look up at the great sky I seem to expand inside; and my spirit becomes very large, akin to the spirit of the sky. Those who are soothsayers, or whatnot, let them answer me with the reason, Why is that?

Then in the distance I saw moving along close to the ground a black little storm. Out of it spat angry, jagged little forks of lightning. And a torrent stood straight between it and the little patch of earth over which it was. And I thought: now the people who are experiencing this storm do not feel that at the moment a little storm is passing over their plot of land, but to them it seems that the universe is in convulsion.

* * * * * * *

Now I am accustomed to having things done

with dispatch. I went into the dining-car for a meal, and I was exasperated, as I always am on dining-cars, by (as it seemed to me) the delinquency of the service. The waiters in a "diner" seem sufficient in proportion to the number of tables to be served. Why does it always take them such an unconscionable time to fetch anything? Particularly was I annoyed this day by the wait for my check. I communicated my displeasure to the gentleman opposite to me. "Well," he said, "you can't possibly go anywhere but on this train; what difference does it make?" I hadn't thought of this; and as I went from the car I pondered the idea.

*　　*　　*　　*　　*　　*　　*

Well, I had it! The reason you want to escape from a dining-car instantly you have eaten is simple enough—because you can't smoke there. Consideration of this infelicity of dining-cars probably it was (turning my thought to evil things), put me in mind of one of the deplorable results of prohibition. And this matter let me consider:

I think it will be found, when the roll is called and (like Colonel Newcome in the dress of the poor gray friars) I answer "adsum," that I, as

[175]

little as (almost) any man, have not failed to place due value on the pleasure of the society of women. Even so, I have always held it as a work of his wisdom that civilized man had fashioned one citadel against their charms, had held one sanctuary to masculinity, one place inviolate —that is, his Club. What havoc then to a mind which had accepted this order of things as beneficent and enduring, immutable, to discover frequently in the Middle West *women in clubs,* excellent clubs! Have they not their own clubs (so called), sacred to their sex? The reason for this new order of things, I was told, was that since the closing of the bars club revenue had so fallen off it had been deemed expedient to open club dining-rooms to women, so to increase patronage there.

* * * * * * *

This narrative has business in Cincinnati, and so I must be getting on to that city. But one of these times I am going to write an article (or maybe it will be a book) about railway journeys, and the excellent things that they are for introducing a man to himself and cementing a friendship founded upon multitudinous interests.

* * * * * * *

MRS. KILMER AT WALNUT HILLS

You wouldn't think that a pleasant city like Cincinnati would harbor such a wicked cabman as there is there. He charged me double what an honest cabman would to drive me from the station to my hotel.

At my hotel they must have thought I was some sort of superstitious gambler. I drew room number 711. And on going to dinner the coatroom girl gave me check number seven.

I saw in the papers that I was to speak "before a gathering of Cincinnati *literati*" in an "auditorium" somewhere down town at two o'clock the next afternoon. Also, I encountered the news that Mrs. Joyce Kilmer was to give a lecture at three o'clock on the same afternoon, at the women's club—wherever that might be. Mrs. Joyce Kilmer? It seemed to me I had heard that name before. Perhaps it was the lady to whose daughter Rose I had stood godfather. Perhaps it was the lady at whose house I had stayed for months on end, time and again. Perhaps this was the widow of Joyce Kilmer—my friend in sickness and in health, in sorrow and in joy, in adversity and in success, now as then first in the house of

my heart, and on whose like I shall never look
again. Perhaps this was Aline!

* * * * * * *

I opened a letter. It began:

"I suppose you are in Cincinnati to-day, and I
hope you are well and comfortable. Your father
and I spent the first week that we were married
in Cincinnati. We stopped at the Burnett
House. That was forty-seven years ago."

You may think that is just a letter; but I will
tell you that is history. "Forty-seven years ago"
Cincinnati was the Athens of the Ohio Valley,
the Paris of the Middle West, a fair and (in that
broad and provincial land) a fabled city, the me-
tropolis (mother) of fashion and of culture.
When I was a boy I heard frequently with wonder (from those who were "traveled") of the
great sights of the world: the "inclined plane"
and the "zoölogical garden" in Cincinnati. And
sometime before I was a boy, frocks that were
distingué were imported, by those who were great
in my part of the world, from Cincinnati.
Thither (to the "conservatory" there) went
those of the young who were of high refinement
for the best education in music to be had, and
thither (William M. Chase among them, and an

uncle of mine, too) went these who would be students of painting, and there, in those days, were published magazines (look them up in the library) of a type of sheer literary excellence better than anything we now have to show.

"Your father and I spent the first week that we were married in Cincinnati." Yes, so it would have been. For all that region round, a generation ago, Cincinnati (soft and lovely name) meant their wedding journey, too.

* * * * * * *

Then it was my old friend, John G. Kidd, of Stewart and Kidd Company, booksellers there, gave a luncheon at the Business Men's Club, a club of excellent appointment.

Enters here one Howard Saxby, the gentleman who is to "introduce" me, a veteran journalist and lecturer (old war-horse sort of character), and a personage I most certainly should not have cared to miss. A man of middle age, generous bulk, and courtly presence: tail coat, braid around the edges; dull red handkerchief in breast pocket; cane; English born, thoroughly Americanized; old friend of Riley; runs *Saxby's Magazine,* writes a brilliant column in the Cincinnati *Commercial-Tribune* headed "Curbstone Gossip," and contributes to this paper a feature called "Saxby's Salmagundi"—"That Tailor's Bill of Mine" appeared while I was there, with "apologies to Riley's 'Old Sweetheart of Mine.'"

Discussed, did Saxby, the recent "foreign invasion" of the United States by our literary brothers from across the waters. His opinion that: "Our authors are rushed too quickly to the front—too soon shelved." And (highly engaging thing) an ardent Dickensian, he. Much incensed by something Walpole had said in one of his Cincinnati lectures. "What the devil did he mean—what right has he got to say that Dickens had no business to write 'Bleak House'?"

Talks like this:

"I have always had difficulty in telling Murray Hill and Booth Tarkington apart. They look so different.

"When one comes to think about it, it really is strange how much alike these litry fellers all look.

"Stephen Leacock looks like a cross between George Bernard Shaw and the late Marshall P. Wilder.

[180]

"Have you ever seen Joseph Hargesheimer? Well, he *reads* all right.

"E. Phillips Oppenheim and Hugh Walpole might well be taken for twins 'in the dark with a light between them.'

"I (myself) was once taken for Henry Watterson, until I proved by showing a receipt that I had settled my tab at the Pendennis Club the night before.

"Christopher Morley has often been mistaken for Mary Roberts Rinehart, and J. M. Barrie and Brander Matthews could use the same knife and fork without knowing the difference—until afterward.

"Hewitt Handsome Howland told me he once gave a royalty check to George Ade, thinking he was giving the certified piece of paper to John Burroughs.

"Richard Le Gallienne strongly objects to being stopped on the street and asked: 'This is Mr. William J. Locke, is it not?'

"Meredith Nicholson (fine, whole-souled chap) is often taken for the lamented Elizabeth B. Browning, especially when driving about Indianapolis in his Ford.

"Maurice Maeterlinck could fill a lecture date

for William Jennings Bryan without any one in the audience distinguishing the difference."

* * * * * * *

Mr. Saxby: "Ladies and gentlemen, this is Mr. Murray Hill. Mr. Hill, this is the audience."

I arose, placed my unfortunate, nickel-plated watch on the table, and delivered my

ADDRESS

* * * * * * *

I don't know how it strikes you, but I'll tell you how it strikes me. I find it somewhat disconcerting. That is this: You are looking down at that impressionist painting of a roomful of faces—which is your "audience." (Looks very much as though Manet had painted it.) Now and then, here and there, a face or figure defines itself more distinctly against, so to say, the canvas; stands out, to put it so, from the frame; then fades again into place. Thus in Cincinnati suddenly appeared vividly before me *several* ancient gentlemen, sitting in a row, obviously very deaf, bending forward, each with hand (like a fan) to his right ear.

I cut my talk fifteen minutes short. Me for

the Woman's Club! Said a lady in the press:
"Are you going to hear Mrs. Kilmer?" She
meant it as a question. I took it as an invitation.
"Yes, indeed," I said; "come!" And I took her
arm and moved her through the throng. I waved
my stick at a waiting taxi across the street before the Sinton. The lady was a bit startled.
She said: "But, you know, I have a family." But,
figuratively speaking, I threw myself on her
like a ton of brick. "That's all right," I replied,
"with me. Where to?" She told the man, and
away we went.

She was a very attractive lady. Youthful and
handsome and engaging in manner. I do not
know her name. Though she became so friendly
as to tell me about several books she had published, she retained her embarrassment throughout the drive.

*   *   *   *   *   *   *

A charming little theater, that interior. The
stage, a frame of soft golden light.

I had never "heard" Mrs. Joyce Kilmer. But
I quite understood that she could not really "lecture." For one thing, she had always been
(throughout the years of my knowledge of her)
altogether a home sort of woman. To dances,

no; I never heard of such a thing! Nor to card parties; I should have been decidedly amazed (not to say shocked) had I *ever* heard of her being at one. About as much of a suffragette as I am. Not a singer, a motorist, a tennis player; the author, occasionally and in a very quiet way, of a beautiful poem, yes; now and then "poured" at the Author's Club, on ladies' day. Reading, very desultory. Her only deep interests: her husband, her children, her house. Though a decoration, indeed, and a very charming presence. It was to me about as congruous to think of her as a traveling lecturer as to think of her as a tight-rope performer.

Then, of course, her voice did not "carry." "Everybody" said so, who had heard her at the outset of her career as a lecturer a couple of years ago. But—she was very brave—and people flocked to hear her (or to see her), of course, because of her fame.

A sudden hush. She had entered back stage, and (a flexible, perfectly symmetrical figure sheened in her frock of black) tripped with a rhythmic, swinging lightness (no one else walks as she) to her chair at the front. While a lady

[184]

who appeared to be much skilled in such Parliamentary matters pronounced a few appropriate preliminary periods, she looked demurely at the floor before her. Her head generously wound in its plaited coils of brown; her features cut like a Grecian marble. (I would admit, if I thought she would forgive me, that I was a bit startled, and then somewhat amused, at how demure the situation made her.)

She stood, very erect, chin slightly tilted, looking far away straight before her, one arm lightly resting across the top of a little reading-stand. Girlhood, she looked, newly come to perfect bloom. She began in a little voice that soared out over that space like a bird high in the sky. It rang clear and sweet like the sound of a silver bell. Dew was on the breath of it, and all manner of fragrant things. Elves were in it, too, innocent mischievous sprites.

She told with a kind of brotherly sympathy, and with some sly amusement, of women who were poets, many of them her personal friends. Her quotations were delivered in a sort of queer, bewitching chant. She was all simplicity—she was all naturalness. Complete was her triumph!

MEN AND BOOKS AND CITIES

As a penetrating critic of art, I was stunned. For this thing which Aline had prepared was consummate.

*   *   *   *   *   *   *

In the evening with Mr. Kidd to a meeting of the Literary Club; an association of one hundred members; oldest organization of its kind, I was told, in the country; entire membership at that time went to the Civil War. In its archives many souvenirs of its venerable years. On the walls of its rooms the book plate of Laurence Sterne, portraits of Goldsmith, Dr. Johnson, and so on, and this legend: "Here comes one with a paper." Members are, undoubtedly, men of substance; and here comes one with a paper dealing, perhaps, with history, or politics, or archeology, or education, or economics, or law, or religion, as likely as with literature.

*   *   *   *   *   *   *

I noticed a thing in my jaunt. This: when anywhere about the country you meet what might be called a real writer—that is, a professional novelist, or, say, a journalist of national reputation, you find that he looks very much like anybody else; he might be a banker, a lawyer, real estate man, commission merchant, hotel proprietor, or anything at all. That's the way I look, too. But when you meet somebody in the advertising business he is very likely to be very literary in effect: large flowing black tie, shell-rimmed eye-glasses, and so on. Tell me about that!

*　　*　　*　　*　　*　　*　　*

I don't know where to say the house is. We started from the upper reaches of Walnut Hills and came down into a district which appeared to be an older part of Cincinnati. Then we could not readily identify the house we sought. There was one which one of my friends thought might be it. A very plain, ordinary house. The porch had been torn away and a box (built, probably, to contain canned goods in shipment) served as a step to the front door. As we got out of the car a little, sparrow-like lady opened the door and gave us welcome.

The lady? Why, I thought I had told you. Mrs. Mary S. Watts, of course. We had a very pleasant call. Nobody said anything of the slightest consequence. While we were talking in came the lady's husband (unaware of any "company") getting some things together for a railway journey. A ruddy, hearty, sportsman-

[187]

like gentleman, to whom you would have taken a decided fancy.

* * * * * * *

I always like a waitress. They are a very human kind of beings. I must tell you about one with whom I became acquainted in Cincinnati. She was a very plump, cheerful person. Told me she worked eleven hours a day, seven days a week. I said, "My goodness!" This seemed to me, in the circumstances, a rather mild exclamation. She replied: "I enjoy it more than anything else I do."

* * * * * * *

I contemplated them a good deal, those men who sit and sit, hour after hour, in hotel lobbies, doing absolutely nothing. There are great numbers of them, everywhere, in every city. Middle aged, most of them, the men I mean, well dressed, well fed. They don't read; they don't talk; they don't appear to be particularly observing the scene. They just sit. And, as George Moore says of some one, their life going by all the while. It may be that they are reflecting on the mystery of their lives. I think that, however, improbable. I think it likely that, if they were asked what they were doing, they would reply that they were waiting for the next train. They might be annoyed if you should tell them that they are also waiting for the last train—for the time when each of them will have a train entirely to his own honor, all the passengers his relatives and friends, and he will ride alone in state in the club car up ahead.

CHAPTER XIII

CHICAGO has been maligned. The world has been deceived about that city. I must set this matter aright.

My last (and only) visit to Chicago before this was at the time of the World's Fair. I went in the charge of my mother. Spacious accommodations were not obtained for me. I remember that I slept in a closet. My principal impression of the city, during the years since, was that they had, in some places, board sidewalks there.

It was night. That is the time to arrive in Chicago. Do just as I did. We (the lady with whom I had traveled from Cincinnati and I) emerged from the Illinois Central Station at Twelfth Street, or, as I believe the block there is called, Park Row. I loaded our things into a cab and we turned into a purring stream of other glow-worm cars up the noble, slightly winding

[190]

stretch of Michigan Avenue, now a far-flung scarf of cool, purple night, embroidered with its stately march of tall-stemmed, yellow-gleaming lamps. Ahead to the left, a symmetrical façade of twinkling windows, the Blackstone; and at the right a deep sense of the city's mighty foil, the Lake.

We paused at the hotel while I signed up. Then on we sped, for the lady was to be taken to where she was to stop with friends far out. As we went I said: "This, indeed, is very beautiful." And so, too, by day. There is a sense of flowing rhythm about that avenue. It breathes distinction and charm. And it does not look like a street anywhere else. It has the *feel* of Chicago.

* * * * * * *

I went round seeing my friends. One of the peculiarities of Chicago is the taste that city displays for youth, slenderness and elegance in its literary editors. There is my friend, young and slender and elegant Henry Blackman Sell, who for long ran the book page of the *Daily News,* succeeded by young and slender and elegant Harry Hanson. And there is my friend, equally young and slender and elegant, Burton

Rascoe, literary editor (until quite recently) of the *Tribune.* And there (but, my goodness! I should in politeness have mentioned her first) is my friend, the even younger, slenderer and more elegant Fanny Butcher, who conducts the "tabloid book reviews" feature of the *Tribune,* and also is the proprietor of the dainty shop, "Fanny Butcher: Books." Llewellyn Jones, literary editor of the *Evening Post,* it is true, looks as though he might be thirty. But that doesn't alter the general situation.

I was glad when Burton said that Keith Preston would be at luncheon, as I had never met him. Now I am not unfamiliar with the society of humorists—but I am not going to say what you think I am. I am not going to say that I have not found the conversation of humorists any funnier than that of any other men. Not at all. The forty or fifty professional humorists of my acquaintance are easily the most humorous men I know.

He appeared at the moment appointed—a thing, I have found, which some humorists don't always do. A smallish, youngish chap, in large spectacles; very modest, very "retiring" in effect; friendly enough in manner, in a quiet way;

and so "soft-spoken" it was difficult to hear him even across a small table. Eccentric, as you might say, as a humorist; in that he says nothing in the slightest humorous. Commented upon this later to a friend of his, and she replied: "He never does." And so, you see, I (supported more or less by Burton) had to supply all the humor of the luncheon.

＊　　＊　　＊　　＊　　＊　　＊　　＊

It was a gray and rather turbulent day as we sped along by the lake. A racing wind dashed our faces with spray, and the white-caps from far out leaped and ran over the choppy surface toward the shore. She quite agreed with me. It always bothers me to be told: "Too bad it isn't a nice day. I did so hope it would be. Yesterday was such a glorious day!" There is not only one kind of a day which is fine. Beauty does not depart from the earth when the blaze of the sun is softened by a veil. What poetry, as the Dutchmen well knew, is in a day hung close to a sky of reverie, in a haze of mauve! There is grandeur, too, an organ-like tune for the spirit, in an angry day. Indeed, I like days of every kind.

＊　　＊　　＊　　＊　　＊　　＊　　＊

"Well, of course," I said, "we have the Hudson."

"Ah! I know," she replied, "but you don't *live* with that the way we do with the lake."

* * * * * * *

They were putting on a "Boost Chicago" campaign. Great streamers flung across the streets read: "The City of Opportunity," and "Throw Away Your Hammer—Go Get a Horn!"

* * * * * * *

He lives (with his wife and several children) somewhere a monstrous way, I gathered, from the office of the *Daily News,* where he writes editorials. Carl Sandburg, I mean. But by putting up for the night at a friend's house he was able to attend the little party in Hyde Park. He went out with me on the train to Fifty-second Street. About as tall as I am (that's rather tall), sturdily built, somewhere in the early forties, hair considerably more than touched with iron gray, face decidedly weather-beaten in effect, furrowed and lined. General impression, a man who has done a good deal of hard work —one who has lived far from softly. Movement, deliberate. Manner, a blend of deep seriousness and of kindness toward all. Not talkative.

Makes no jests, and does not respond with anything like hilarity to your jokes.

I heard a delightful lady speak of him in a most motherly and affectionate tone of voice as looking "like an amiable second-story man."

We were obliged to stand in the train, and there was little opportunity for conversation. Walking away from the suburban station I discovered by some chance that he is very fond of Belloc.

He made a valiant effort to carve the meat (the honor of which function I wisely declined), but could not grasp the principle of how he should go as to grain, and finally gave it up.

After being much urged, he took from his pocket a few manuscript poems (rather soiled and worn in look) and read them, without any effort at stage play. I asked him for these poems to be considered for THE BOOKMAN. He agreed; but I forgot to take them when we parted, and he did not remind me of the matter.

Excellent, remarkably so, book stores of every character in Chicago.

* * * * * * *

Undoubtedly the worst place to eat in, that city, anywhere in the world.

*   *   *   *   *   *   *

Mr. Doran's telegram read: "E. V. Lucas at the Blackstone; introduce yourself." At the hotel desk I was handed a card: the gentleman's name, and, as is the fashion with Englishmen, neatly engraved in the lower left-hand corner the name of his club, the Athenæum; written in pencil, "I'll be in till half past seven." I got him on his room telephone. "At the stand where the newspapers are. I'll be there," he said. We went down through all those labyrinthian little lobbies to the grill for dinner.

You are, doubtless, familiar with portraits of him. Had I not known his picture so well I certainly should not have taken this to be E. V. Lucas, or, indeed, a man who had anything at all to do with literature. A youngish fifty, perhaps. Rather tall. A good weight, not over heavy. Light on his feet, like a man who has taken his share in active field games. Something of a stoop. A smile, good, natural, but sly. Dark hair, shot with gray. Noble prow of a nose. Most striking note of all, that ruddy complexion, ruddy to a degree which (as I reflect upon the matter) seems to be peculiar to a certain type of Englishman.

He studied the card with deep attention. Evidently not a man (as I am) who eats carelessly, regarding one thing (if good of its kind) as about as good as another. Ordered an excellent meal. Very particular as to the manner in which dishes were served. Much annoyed that the waiter did not instantly replace the silver cover upon the dish from which he had just served the roast beef. Spoke to him sharply because he was withdrawing from the table when something else remained to be done. Amazed at the indifference of the man, who (I suppose Mr. Lucas did not know) was going to strike on the day after the morrow, and probably held all diners in scorn. Topped off with a very handsome strawberry shortcake.

He had been in Chicago several days and had not made himself known to any one, except at Marshall Field's book store, which he spoke of as the finest book store within his knowledge. Had come from the Orient by the way of San Francisco. California? "Most beautiful place I ever saw." Curious to hear all that might be said concerning recent literary visitors from

England. Appeared to be much amused at the
number of them. Was interested to learn the
standing over here of English writers who had
taken up residence in the United States years
ago—to name one, Richard Le Gallienne. Inquired if they had become naturalized American
citizens. Was considerably put out because he
had not been able to buy any of the books of
Edith Wharton since his arrival in this, her own,
country. (I offered the paper shortage and
other difficulties present in American publishing
as my country's apology.)

He said: "I think she is about the best there
is in England or America."

He continued to look at me rather severely in
the matter of our failure to appreciate Mrs.
Wharton. Indeed, his manner (I reflected with
some amusement) might imply that he held me
personally responsible for everything over here
of which he did not approve. We spoke of a
recent visitor here for whose work neither of us
cared. "You bought his books," said Mr. Lucas.
Not *I!* "*You* have pretty well ruined things
over here with your prohibition." He used to
look forward to a meal; but now . . . ! I has-
tened to assure him that in the matter of the

Eighteenth Amendment I was quite (Oh! quite) guiltless. And "*you* are easily pleased with your comic supplements." In broad American humor, I was charmed to hear, he liked very much Walt Mason, and Mutt and Jeff. Don Marquis he thought (rightly enough) our best columnist.

He made a couple of horribly bad puns. I can't for the life of me recollect them.

He liked my Tarkington story about "Hamlet." "There's a good deal in the Belasco idea, too," he said. "I like to think of Shakespeare as a practical man." As to the many merits of slang, he denied them. On the ground that it was a jargon of stock phrases. "In speaking, as in writing," he reasoned, "what one should seek is an individual, a fresh rearrangement of words." Now there is a good deal to be said, both thus and so, as to this matter; but (and I couldn't think of less space for the subject) I cannot take up a chapter here for the subject.

When he had finished a cigar or two he took from his pocket a very worn-looking, cloth-covered cigarette case and dumped from it a cigarette onto the palm of one hand.

[199]

He commented on the cost of living in Chicago. "Just think of that, nearly three pounds a night for a bed-room!" The other evening he had gone "out" for his dinner, to a place he had observed earlier in the day, and which, from the look of it, in England would have been very "reasonable." "And everything was about one-third more than here." Asked how he would find the situation in New York.

Discussed publishing. "Not much risk" about a book, he said, "when everything gets published and when people buy anything." He, as well as I, it seems, had written what the trade terms "jacket copy," that is the advertising matter describing a book which goes on its paper wrapper. "You have here such a number of words which make it easy, words which mean so much, and mean nothing at all, like cave-man and mother love."

We made an appointment to meet at breakfast. He was leaving for the East shortly before noon the following day.

* * * * * * *

I was, he told me, to be one of the party. Mr. and Mrs. Hahner were coming for him in their car and take him for a drive until time for his train. He would, of course, call her Mrs. Hahner (which has recently become her name), but she is known to all the rest of the world by her maiden name of Marcella Burns, presiding genius of the Marshall Field book store.

In that Louis Seize lobby he crammed a charge of tobacco into a very old-looking pipe, and remarked that he was sorry he had not "met" us before, as he had wished he "could find somebody to go to the music halls with." "Us" (or we) being, presumably, the Hahners and me—the extent, as you might say, of his "circle" in Chicago. And the only "music hall" there with which I myself am acquainted is the Marigold Gardens, where I went with a remarkably interesting lady, about whom (when this History is finished) I expect to write a novel. It will probably be called "The Yellow Slippers."

This was the first time I had seen him got up for out-of-doors. He wore a soiled sport hat, very light in color, the material of which I can best describe as resembling cat fur; a stringy muffler, also light in color; a wrinkled rain-coat, and beneath this a detachable woolen lining or under coat. Unlike most Englishmen, he did

[201]

not (at any time I saw him) carry a stick. He told me that he "always froze to death" on motor car drives.

There was a light rain when we started; the top was up, and he was assigned to the front seat with George Hahner, to give him the better view. Here he appeared to enjoy himself hugely in a very animated discussion of baseball throughout the trip. Though he contended that cricket was the better sport, there is no doubt he was considerably "hipped" by our game. Had been going by himself since he got to the States. Went to a Sunday game in San Francisco.

Back by the hotel to take on his luggage. He had been saying apologetically that there was "a good deal of it." But Mrs. Hahner, whose *forte* is to make everybody happy, had as repeatedly declared there was plenty of room for it all. Men began bringing it out, and what they brought was stowed away in the car. A lull then in the proceedings, and everybody (not owning the property) stout-heartedly affirmed that that was no amount of luggage at all. With that sly Lucas smile: "Oh! there's more to come."

It was one of those outwardly dingy-looking stations in the interior of Chicago. We drove up at the side, and as an attendant loaded Mr. Lucas's traveling equipment onto a little hand-truck, I made this inventory of the outfit:

SEVEN THINGS

1. Steamer trunk.
2. Cardboard hat box.
3. Suitcase.
4. Army roll.
5. Laundry bag, half filled.
6. Umbrella.
7. Bag containing some sort of clubs, too short for golf sticks; probably cricket bats.

Indeed, he had eight things; he carried in his hand a parcel (in shape suggesting books) *done up in a piece of newspaper*.

"All a-board!" We stood with him in a group by the steps of his coach. The little truck had not arrived. What was to be done! Then the station attendant was seen propelling his vehicle down the platform at a rattling clip. Mr. Lucas rapidly shook hands round the circle, turned and sprang up the steps—an odd, a humorous and a memorable figure: stoop, smile, whitish hat, and long coat flowing out after him. A bevy of porters hustled his collection of things aboard. **The** train began to move; and only four people in Chicago knew that this particular and very distinguished English man of letters had ever been there.

* * * * * * *

What she said to me was these words: "Murray, you are *funny* if you *are* silly." I do not know what she meant. I was revolving in my mind the question: Who painted her? Rossetti could not have done it, because he was a rotten bad painter. And yet she has what I suppose you might call a Rossetti mouth. I said to her: "I must go. I'll be back." She said to me: "When will you be back? Yesterday you said you would be back, and you did not come." I said to her: "And cn Sunday, Katherine, you were to take me to the dunes—and you merely took 'Walking-Stick Papers.'" She said to me: "I'll have everything straightened up when you come." I said to her: "Within an hour." Rich lashes covered her eyes, as she looked toward the floor. I took up my hat and stick. Her bosom was gently rising and falling. I made a step toward the door. She looked up. A diamond gleamed in each of her eyes.

"Whyinhell don'tcher watch out where yore goin'!" yelled State Street taxi driver.

"Brother," I said to him, "pardon me. I was thinking: Who painted her? Do you suppose it would have been Renoir?"

"Poor fish!" said taxi man. Even so.

   *   *   *   *   *   *   *

"Well," I said to Fanny Butcher, "the artist makes copy out of passion."

"I know an artist," said Fanny Butcher, "who makes passion out of copy."

A bright child, is Fanny Butcher.

CHAPTER XIV

MATERNITY AND CLIMATE

I REMEMBER Mr. Lucas had said to me: "What! Can you write in a hotel room?" I see no reason why one should not be able to write in any kind of a room. So voluminous were the pages of copy on my table at one of the hotels where I had been that I thought it but polite to explain to the maid what I was up to. She was a very fat negress who bore the blooming name of Rose. "I'm writing a book," I said.

"Must be hard work," she replied; "it would be for me." Then she very graciously added: "I bet that's a good book to *read*."

No, Mr. Lucas had said, he could not write in hotel rooms; but he had no difficulty in writing on trains. I had looked forward to getting considerable writing done during my three days and a half on the Overland Limited. Found I couldn't write at all. I must examine into the psychology of this matter when I have the time.

* * * * * * *

I can't shave on trains, either. The reason for this is that I use the old-fashioned, muzzle-loader type of razor; and I can't sway with the roll of the craft. . . . Each morning I climbed into the barber's chair up ahead. The train would be sailing smoothly along. The barber would elaborately lather me. The train would begin to slow up. He would start with my cheek. Train stopped. He had got around to my throat. Bang! Coupling cars. Deftly he had jerked away his razor-hand. Makes another attempt. Again, bang! . . . a shock that nearly smashes the train.

He worked over me, day after day, both as a barber and as a missionary. He would have me a convert in California, even before I got there. And so I was "from New York?" Well, he knew a man who had six children—five of them born in California, "without any trouble." The sixth was born in New York; and the birth of this child nearly cost the life of the gentleman's wife. Indeed, he only "saved her by the skin of his teeth." Shows the effect of climate.

"The scientific part of it," concluded the barber, "I don't know. But," he added, "he thought too much of her to lose her for that."

MEN AND BOOKS AND CITIES

I was repeatedly and positively assured that residence in California would "add ten years" to my life.

    *   *   *   *   *   *   *

I came across him in the vestibule. He was waiting for a seat at dinner. Little, old fellow; flannel shirt, wizened, stooped, iron spectacles: so unprosperous in appearance I was rather surprised that he should be going in to dinner at all . . . you might have expected him to eat his dinner from a cardboard box. He was very much provoked because he had not received the attention and courtesy which he thought was his due from the manager of the dining-car, and (thus we became acquainted) began to grumble to me concerning this.

We were seated at the same table. He inquired (he had a worn looking volume in his hand) if I was "much of a reader." I told him that I should not say that I was "much of a reader," but that I read a little now and then to pass the time away. He handed me his book. It was: "Robbery Under Arms: a Story of Life and Adventure in the Bush and in the Goldfields of California," by Rolf Boldrewood, imprinted 1889. He declared it was one of the best "dime

[208]

novels" ever written. Our discussion became literary. Another of his favorite volumes (he informed me) was "Moby Dick." He had greatly enjoyed "The Education of Henry Adams." Suddenly he asked: "Are you a New Englander? Well," was his comment, "you couldn't, then, savor the flavor of the humor of the book." It developed that, in his way, he was a collector. He had "a fairly complete library" in two subjects: gypsies and sleight-of-hand.

He asked if I had been much in the Pacific Islands. His home was in Boston; and he was on his way to Hawaii, having business interests in Honolulu. He told me a good deal about the volcano there; but remarked that no amount of description could give one any idea of it. Chiefly, however, he discussed the "delicate" dishes of the islands, "delicious" foods. He looked like an exceedingly weather-beaten gargoyle.

* * * * * * *

I remember some time ago hearing several old gentlemen in a club in New York discuss a recent violent thunderstorm. Said one: "I don't mind a thunderstorm in the day time. Indeed, I rather like to hear one come up. But I have an objection to being struck by lightning in the middle of the night—I don't want to meet my Maker with my things all about my head." Precisely! I have very much the same feeling every time I go to bed on a train. I see a mental picture of myself being dug out from under an awful wreck and most ridiculously attired for a scene of tragedy.

Another thing. I was surprised every morning that we had not been held up by bandits during the night. I altogether fail to understand why trains are not held up every day while crossing those plains and mountains, where not a moving thing is to be seen for half a day at a time. I hesitate to encourage banditry by so highly recommending one form of robbery beyond another. But it certainly does seem to me that any company issuing insurance to highwaymen (if such companies there be) would much prefer to take a chance on a couple of gentlemen about to roll a log across the track in the Sierra Nevada mountains, with a perfectly free getaway on all sides, than on any one of the numerous automobile parties of adventurous spirits who undertake

MATERNITY AND CLIMATE

My new acquaintance (I met him in the club car reading a volume of O. Henry) said that he was exceedingly sorry we had not met earlier in the journey. He repeated this regret several times. He had had a very dull trip. The reason for this, he explained, was that he, like myself, did not really "make up with everybody." He kept himself a good deal to himself; and that, he acknowledged to me, was the kind of a man he liked to know. He gave me his card. He would not have given his card to just anybody.

In one of those extremely handsome ferries that they have here we went across the Bay together—that noble bay, sea-gulls wheeling (with their wild cries) above us as we went.

CHAPTER XV

THE literary editor of this newspaper (San Francisco Chronicle) has got a woman to do an evil thing. I highly approve of his conduct in this. The scandalous affair is as follows:

Perceiving by instinctive intelligence that he himself dared not enter into my presence with his corrupt proposal (I am a very savage man and have destroyed more than one wicked literary editor merely by a glance) he played upon that weakness of mine, which, though I endeavor to conceal it, I fear is notorious. He knew (whether through knowledge of my reputation at home, or whether by low cunning, I cannot say) that, though I am a roarer among men, I am as a toy in the hands of feminine beauty, a slave before the eyes of a lovely lady.

So what does he do, this fellow? He discovers (by some gum-shoe method) that there is in this city a lady who not long ago lived next door

[214]

to me in *New York* and (*deeply I felt it*) filled all that neighborhood with charm. He has her ring me up at my hotel. He has her instill into my mind an idea. The idea that (busy as *I* am with my vacation here) *I* write something for this paper. *I* am glad that evidently the thought did not occur to him to have her beguile me to do this: give up the six weeks of my vacation still coming to me and go do his work on the paper while he finished out my vacation himself.

"*Certainly*," *I* said; "*certainly, delighted, with pleasure, nothing could make me happier!*" *I* said; and *I* leaned limp against the wall. *I* wonder, *I* thought, what *I* have let myself in for now? *You* have no idea, my dears, what ladies have let me in for before this. One time, *I* remember— but that would take too long to tell; and also, doubtless, it would be unwise for me to go into the matter. Anyhow, *I* got out of it all right. But the experience has taught me nothing. *Very* likely *I'd* do the same thing over again. And, indeed, *I'm* glad of that.

But where was *I?* Oh, yes! "*What*," *I* asked, "*shall I write about?*" *I* felt decidedly gloomy; *I* fancied *I'd* be required to tell all about literature. *I've* told all about literature any number *of times. And it seems to me the matter ought to be let go at that. What else, please tell me, is there to be said?*

"Why, write about yourself," rippled the voice over the wire. I cheered up immensely. Now, a lot of people hem and haw when they are asked to talk about themselves. They think they should pull all the proper modesty stuff before they begin. You never catch me at that sort of bunk-um. When anybody encourages me to talk about myself, she (just sort of slipped off my pen, the word "she") has got nothing else to do the rest of the afternoon but just sit back and listen.

Well, I was rather cleverly introduced to an audience in Cincinnati a few weeks ago as a person "born in Indiana but who had never been west of the Hudson river." And, in a manner of speaking, this, until recently, was so enough. Though the house where I was born is "still standing" in Indianapolis, I went to New York (to become a painter) at about the age of nine-teen, and have lived there mainly during the ten or twelve years since—though some ill-natured people say that I look almost thirty-five. (It is astonishing what malice some people have!)

Now, however, man and boy I have lived in

TO SAN FRANCISCO

San Francisco since 7:30 o'clock in the evening of May 9, 1920. And, slowly but surely, I have become (what you call 'em?) a San Franciscoac. I certainly have.

You see, I've got a dog at home, very valuable young man, by name Tristram Shandy, Gentleman. And he is being boarded out only temporarily. I'll have to return and get him, and then I'll be back.

My love! brightest and most alluring of maidens among all the world's cities; San Francisco, enchantress and darling! it will be but as a moment that I am torn from your gleaming arms! Your fragrance will caress me the time I am away.

Golden lady! take me, and by your great beauty will I become a writer that can really write.

Dear, wait for me here!

* * * * * * *

When I left the *Chronicle* office I went over to the *Bulletin.* But first I should tell you how I got to the *Chronicle.* Among the pleasantest things in the world to the senses are the public squares, garnished with greenery, of a first-rate city. More delightful by far (to me) than that city's imposing parks. Well, when I would come out of my hotel of a morning Union Square was there at the door to blow me a welcome to the day. Semi-tropical Union Square with its dress-parade row of sturdy date-palms before me. (And as I would go home at night I'd see the lights across the little way strung like lanterns through the trees.)

First, I'd take a turn about the square, and its neighborhood, looking up those streets to the North and West of it, those broad, shining, speckless San Francisco streets. Streets descending their steep hills, in a series of terraces, block by block, and their gleaming car-tracks coming like a cascade down the middle. Then I'd turn, through that sparkling city toward Market Street. At "newspaper corners" I'd pause to revel in the Piccadilly-Circus-like banks of color of the flower venders. And I'd stand and muse before one of those amazingly provincial news-stands at the curb. Take, at random, one of these little shacks of boards anywhere up or down the street and make a memorandum. You will there (in all likelihood) find on display, among other periodicals, these publications:

TO SAN FRANCISCO

The Nautical Gazette
Asia
The Poultry Journal
Popular Science
Soviet Russia
The Bill Board
New York Clipper
London Times
London Daily Mail
Manchester Guardian
Belfast Weekly News
Cork Examiner
L'Italia
British Californian
El Norte Americano
The Fleet Review
The American Boy
Dramatic Mirror
Police Gazette
American Echo
New Yorker Staats Zeitung
Sydney Morning Herald
Sydney Referee
Auckland Weekly News
Wellington Press
Stockholm's Dagblod

Liberator
Commodore
Orchard and Farm
The National Labor Digest
Daily Sporting Times
Western Worker
The Survey
London Daily Mirror
John Bull
Glasgow Herald
Dublin Freeman
Danish Politikan
El Heraldo de Mexico
Philippines Free Press
The Wireless Age
Birth Control Review
Baseball Magazine
Mothers
South American
Berliner Tageblatt
Sydney Bulletin
Sydney Truth
Melbourne Australasian
Otago Witness
Irish World
Texas Oil Gazette

New Zealand Herald

*   *   *   *   *   *   *

He looked up over his typewriter at me blankly as I entered his little quarters partitioned off.

from the general office of the *Bulletin*. I had noticed that the legend on his door read, "Editorial Writers," and beneath that was printed, "George Douglas." I knew nothing of the man except that I had been told I should "see" him.

"Well, I declare!" he exclaimed. "I thought you were a book agent, and was going to throw you out."

"So I am," I replied. "I want to sell you a copy of the celebrated volume, now in course of preparation, 'Men and Books and Cities.' "

We fell to talking of a number of writer friends of mine who, I here began to discover, have much popularity on the coast: Booth Tarkington, William McFee, Christopher Morley, and A. Edward Newton. Then, of English authors: Chesterton, Belloc, and the lot. And so Lucas had also pussyfooted into (and out of) San Francisco—Douglas was amazed to learn that he had recently been here.

Leaped out, Douglas, to bring in the owner of the paper—that's the way they do in San Francisco—R. A. Crothers. A fine, hearty, ruddy, mountain of an elderly man. He remarked, by way of apology to the visitor, that life in San Francisco was rather "flat" since "the booze had gone." And I discovered that he had pride in the very un-newspaper-like idea that the *Bulletin* printed the line of goods stamped "literature" when it could get it, John Cowper Powys, and others who regard themselves as of letters contributing to its columns.

But wait! (the fellow had been "very busy" when I went in). A man we must lay hold of right away. Frisbee. Got him on the wire. Lunch. Right O!

* * * * * * *

Luncheon party: G. G. Frisbee, prosperous San Francisco druggist. An excellent amateur of books. Happiest man I have ever seen. Got up in very becoming gay checks. Mr. Frisbee's young man son. A lawyer whose name escaped me at the introduction. Mr. Douglas, native of Sydney; places of former residence, South Africa, London, Alaska; a critic, polished, erudite, keenly sensitive to literature, eloquent in talk. Captain Woodside, retired, learned ship building trade in Belfast with Harlon and Wolff, master in sail and steam. Lives in a house on a height, studio window to his den at the top, where surrounded by his instruments he sits and observes through his binoculars the Pacific. Taken up reading as a pastime.

Place: Sub-surface eating place in the business district. Vast area. Used to be called the Bismarck, changed ˙ to its present name, the States, when "Liberty cabbage" was the vogue. Vaulted ceiling done in dainty stenciled frescoes of the German Renaissance, depicting artistry appropriate to the years preceding the drought. Mottoes and inscriptions on ceiling and walls soon to be meaningless. "Prosit!"

Dishes: Delightful sea foods strange to me.

Captain Woodside had just read Conrad's "Nigger of the Narcissus." "Not nearly so good," he declared, "as Marryat." Astonishment round the table. "It's not sea-faring," asserted the captain. General outcry. Passionate (and amazingly detailed) presentation by Douglas of who Conrad is.

Captain totally unmoved. Doggedly reiterates that the book is "not sea-faring." Explains: "Ship goes on her beam's end. Stays so for a day and a half. It righted. Proceeds on her course as though nothing had happened. No allowances made for the shifting of her cargo, which must have occurred with her a day and a half on her beam's end. Any sailor man knows that." He concluded: "A picture ship."

Mr. Hill: "Yes; but literature is full of instances where a writer who certainly should have known what he was talking about has been 'called' by some one who knew intimately the life he described. Kipling, for one outstanding instance, and the clamor he occasioned by his India."

Mr. Douglas: "Quite so, indeed! As just one point:

> On the road to Mandalay,
> Where the flyin'-fishes play.

Mandalay is an inland town, five miles from the coast. No such animals anywhere near as flying-fishes. Also:

> An' the dawn comes up like thunder onter
> China 'crost the Bay!

No bay there. Other side of Mountains."

But Captain Woodside was still on the subject of the Narcissus. And here I got a quick glimpse into the caste of the sea—the drawing of the line, by an old-time skipper, between the quarter-deck and the man before the mast. (A beautiful professional point.) He was saying, the captain: "Several hundred pages about a sick *foc'stl* hand, and a nigger at that!"

The talk turned to the original of London's "Sea Wolf." Well-known figure round San Francisco, it seems, up till a few years ago. Thus he was drawn for me: Looked like anything but a sea-farer. Conveyed the idea of a "Salvation Army Man." Prince Albert coat; broad-brimmed, black felt hat; long, flowing, dark mustaches. Professional smuggler. Revenue officers after him for years; they knew perfectly well what he was doing; he knew that they knew it; never able to "connect him up" with anything. Dare-devil of the deep—strangely ironic end. Met his death in a few inches of water, by a pier: got drunk, asleep rolled off a small boat.

*　*　*　*　*　*　*

After luncheon, with Mr. Frisbee and his son round "the Peninsula" in a car. (Mr. Frisbee, splendid man! so happy all the while I found him difficult to keep up with. How are you going to be roaringly happy every minute straight along for seven hours at a stretch?) Though almost everything (except the kind of thing I tell you) *has* been told about San Francisco (and all California), I have not seen the fact (as I believe it to be) mentioned, that in Golden Gate Park is the only monument to Cervantes in America—a bronze bust above stone pedestal, with bronze figures of the immortal knight and his immortal squire making obeisance before it. Sculptor: Molera de Cebrian (I don't vouch for the spelling). Monument presented to the city (I understand) by an old Spanish grandee of San Francisco. At the roads summit of Twin Peaks we wound about and before us, glinting in the rich sunshine, the city lay "like a jeweled mantle thrown carelessly over many peaks" far below. (Words in quotes from Inez Haynes Irwin's scintillating little volume, "The Californiacs.")

*   *   *   *   *   *   *

Every time you look around in San Francisco there seems to be a bookstore. First time I looked around it was the place of Paul Elder and Company—here commonly called "Paul Elder's." A shop of the pleasant attractiveness of design you would expect to find inhabited by the man who got up the format of the Paul

Elder books—though I do not mean to at all imply that the atmosphere of estheticism is here laid on with a trowel.

Very pleasant man, Mr. Elder. Comfortable size, as you might say, to look at; plump, affable, neat mustache foil to a round face; like his shop—everything in excellent taste, nothing eccentric. In his guest book I signed my name thus, "Murray Hill, New York City, In good health," on a page already inscribed as follows:

Yone Noguchi. Nakano. Happy to return to California.
Hugh Walpole. Garrick Club, London. Delighted to be here at last!
Coningsby Dawson. New York.
Oliver Lodge, England. Full admiration for this great State.

I referred to Mr. Elder's place as a shop. He has the whole of a little building. One of the upper floors constructed as a lecture room. Here had recently appeared, in Saturday afternoon talks: Peter Clark Macfarland, Dr. Henry Frank, and Frederick O'Brien, among others. Being now a veteran of the game, Murray Hill very cheerfully signed up, at Mr. Elder's courteous invitation, to talk there at an early date "on authors he had met and other gossip of the publishing offices." Gossiping in Elder's I learned that Coningsby Dawson had just bought a place at San Diego. And Theodore Dreiser, I heard, was at present writing in Los Angeles.

Coming out of Mr. Elder's, I saw across the street that excellent department store here called the White House, concerning the spacious book section of which I had heard much. And after my call there, pointed back toward my home, the Plaza, I again caught the scent of books. Across what in London would be called a little court from Paul Elder's (and what in Indianapolis would be called a little alley—and in Paris probably a *cul-de-sac*) is the Old Book Shop. A place of really distinctive character, dealing mainly in collectors' volumes.

And there, right around the Square from my hotel, and also overlooking the little Park, I saw the place of A. M. Robertson, here commonly called "Robertson's." Had been told I should see him. A wise man it was, and a very friendly one, who told me that.

Mr. Robertson (popularly hailed, I soon discovered, as "Alec") is a gentleman who has relished life for a very fair span of years. The only deaf person, as well as I can recollect, I ever enjoyed talking with. Leaving his son in charge of the excellent store: "We'll go to lunch." Round to the Bohemian Club, known all over for its annual Grove Play and its elaborate and distinctive manner of entertaining visiting literary personages. Palatial place, its home; vast rooms, spacious as the Reform Club, of London.

We ate at the "kickers' table," where (I was informed) nobody ever likes anything that anybody else says. I got into a great row with a most admirable young man on the subject of printing. Very much against, I was at the moment, the William Morris school. Couldn't "see" at all the kind of printer who thinks, apparently, that a writer was brought into the world in order to give him an opportunity of making a decorative page—a thing to capture the eye, to the subordination of the writer's appeal to the mind. Though I admitted that as you couldn't read Chaucer anyhow, it was all right for the printer, as much as he pleased, to regard him as a *motif* for a pattern in black and white. Jolly time all round!

Afterward, to a little ceremony, the unveiling and dedication of a painting presented to the Bohemian Club by several of its members, who desired their names to be not known. When the club flag fell the picture revealed was a large canvas by Jules Pages, "Sur les Quais, Paris," exhibited at the Paris Salon, 1913, and at the Palace of Fine Arts of the Exposition of 1915. M. Pages, present, made a charmingly diffident speech.

I was (by the courtesy of Mr. Robertson) much at the Club after this. Thursday nights now (before I forget to mention it) they put on excellent entertainments there: songs, and music, stories and recitations; an innovation to keep up joviality since—well, you know, just *since*.

*   *   *   *   *   *   *

Funniest, nicest things to ride on you ever saw. Clutch pole before you with your knees. You sit facing outward, you know. San Franciscoians become so expert they don't have to hold on. Whirl up hill and down dale, shoot around corners. Something like one of those jazz rides at Coney Island. And all the time the man behind you working like fury, pushing and pulling

[229]

those crazy-looking, huge levers. The cable-cars, I mean. And, funny thing! they look exactly like the pictures of that new invention called a cable-car which I used to see in *St. Nicholas* when I was a small boy, and when the only sort of a public street conveyance I had ever seen in real life was a "mule-car."

* * * * * * *

There at my hotel was rotund, jovial Wallace Irwin, who had paid me the honor of a call. He had just got back, he said, from a trip in his "bug wagon," collecting "Jap stuff" in the back country.

* * * * * * *

Seems to me like a foolish remark. But they go on making it. "Another lovely day!" What's the use of saying this, when one day is just like another? When one day is just like another, until a very temperamental young lady I know (who says the California climate is "not moody enough") declares that she wants "to smash that azure sky."

You might just as well say to some one in San Francisco: "See that beautiful woman passing there!" Would be just as much point to such an observation. I tell you, old man, I got so I positively yearned to see, round somewhere, a woman who *was not* beautiful. I'm afraid, however, I should have rushed forward and kissed her, for her dear, pathetic homeliness' sake! But I 'spect the beauty of California women has been press-agented enough.

CHAPTER XVI

A PAL OF JACK LONDON

AND so I went over to the office of the *Call*. A young man there named Mr. Hoffman I wanted to see. In he takes me to see the editor, Fremont Older. Couple of other chaps come along. And we all talk a while. Fremont Older! What a beautiful name (had just such a man not owned it) it would have been for a novelist to have thought of for just such a figure —looks (Mr. Older) like a picture, by a first-rate illustrator, in a popular magazine of a veteran, graft-fighting newspaper man. "He has put," one of my companions told me, "more of our best citizens in jail than anybody else in town." Has been associated in his career with various San Francisco papers. Lives on a ranch, fifty miles out. Commutes.

He remarked, by way of apology to the visitor, that life in San Francisco was "pretty flat" now that "the old days of booze" were past.

[232]

A PAL OF JACK LONDON

What was it I liked so much about San Francisco? Well, I tried to tell him. Has (to my mind) more the look and the *feel* of a first-rate city than any place to be found after you cross the Hudson River headed West. And yet it is, comparatively, tiny. Can walk from one end of Market Street to the other, and back again, in an easy stroll. A city that has somewhat the effect, to employ something of a conceit, of a plaster model of a city on view at an exhibition of the Architectural League. A metropolitan, a cosmopolitan, a great city in miniature.

MR. OLDER: "Maybe one reason is that it never was a town. Sprang up a city. Now when I was in Buffalo not long ago I remember it struck me as very town-like."

It was the "old Palace Hotel," according to Older, that first made San Francisco known all over the world. In Switzerland he had heard: "Oh! yes; that's where the Palace Hotel is." The intention of the original owners had been to make the finest hotel on earth. Had never considered transportation facilities into the city, or anything like that. Dining in rooms, whole turkey always served; what wasn't eaten never touched

[233]

again, thrown away; next guest, new turkey; amorous waste—spirit of the old "flush days."

So out to lunch at the Palace. A dozen others turn up at the table. Come and go without formality. Among them John Barry (a gentleman bearing a marked resemblance to John Drew), prominent feature story writer here, who turns out to be a close friend of Charlie Towne and everybody else "back East."

MR. HOFFMAN: "All rules of journalism are violated here: editors sit down with the business office."

MURRAY HILL: "So long as the editors do not corrupt the business office I suppose it's all right."

I hear much affectionate reminiscence of "famous" old saloons. One among them in particular, The Bank Exchange, kept by one Duncan Nicol, and hallowed by memories of Mark Twain, Bret Harte and Stevenson, who had his individual lemon-squeezer there.

I have now to explode a monstrous fallacy. That the Californian (native or by adoption) never ceases rooting for California except when he is asleep is an idea that flourishes all over the map. The disease, Californoia, is swatted in all the books. Let me set the matter right.

Mr. Hoffman is glad I came when I did, in early Spring. He describes the "drying up" of the country within the next few weeks. Says so many tourists from the "green East" who come "fed up" with "Chamber of Commerce glories" are disappointed. Flowers expected; everything brown. "Now's the time!"

Nope! Modesty with 'em (with the San Franciscoians, at any rate) is almost a vice. Apologize for everything. Cringe and crawl about. Water front? Suppose it will seem pretty small after that of New York—but would you mind looking at it? Or, morning after morning, this: "Pity it isn't a nicer day," some one says. "What's the matter with it?" you ask— as beautiful a day as you ever saw in your life. "Oh! there's rather a high wind." High wind? Pooh! On Manhattan Island, 'twould be no wind at all.

"But all that," a sly one tells me, "is just their way of drawing your fire."

* * * * * * *

Went to see S. Coryn, editor of *The Argonaut*. Wanted to get a sketch of him for my gallery. Found him in, but too hoarse with a cold to talk, or even to whisper.

* * * * * * *

I did not see any of the great collections on the coast, about which much more should be written than is generally known, even among well-informed bookmen. But I did not have to seek diligently to find gentlemen whose avocation is collecting, within the range of merely prosperous means (but with love, science and erudition in the art), fine and rare books. Mr. Young, of the California and Hawaiian Sugar Refining Company, is such a one. Another, a Dr. Robertson (distinguished, I believe, as a specialist in mental and nervous disorders, retired), whisked me one day out to his home at the apex of Russian Hill; where, from his library constructed on the roof, we looked out over the city and the bay; while he elaborated his entertaining theory that Bacon was a paranoiac; and we discussed his Caxtons, Moxons, his copies of the first, second, third and fourth editions of the "Rubaiyat," his horn books, New England primers, his Thackeray and "Pickwick" in original parts, and the lore of "states," and typographical errors of bibliographical significance.

* * * * * * *

[236]

A PAL OF JACK LONDON

They called him "Finn," short for Phineas. Frolic (pronounced Frowlick) was his surname, and frolic was his nature. Frolic, too, was what it meant, his name (I understand), in the language of his native country. A Norwegian. Sculptor by profession. Had designed, Mr. Douglas informed me, "miles" of sculpture at the San Francisco Exposition. But the occupation of sculptor is, one perceives, an intermittent one—there are not miles of monuments to be built every day. And so Finn was at present engaged in constructing a "studio" for Mr. Douglas behind his house in the suburb of Burlingame. I should have called it a library, myself, or a study. But out here they prefer to call anything of the kind a studio.

Stalwart, jovial, garbed in the costume of a laborer, with the heart of a boy, given to joyous bursts of merriment at every mishap, Finn took Douglas and me for a drive in his decidedly dilapidated Ford. As we rattled along the wonderful avenues of eucalyptus I heard the story of his humorous car.

Somewhere at a distance from San Francisco Finn had read "The Sea Wolf," and determined that he must go to see an author so much after his own heart. London at once took a fancy to Frolic—the right type. The two quickly became close friends. Gambling with London the sculptor won a cow and three goats. He kept the cow (or rather the cow kept him) for a number of years. Finally, however, he declared: "What's the good of a cow? One must keep up with the times." And he traded his cow for the Ford.

We passed the house of Stewart Edward White; which, I was told, had been "built by books," that is a new wing, or room, having been added from time to time to the original structure as the author published a new book. A long, low, rambling dwelling (my impression), largely obscured from our vision by a gigantic oak tree before the door.

* * * * * * *

"Yes," George Douglas was saying, "Chicago, or some other place like that in the East."

Certainly a brilliant commutation scene, as we waited for the nine something, Monday morning train to "the city"—always "the city," San Francisco, to the Californian. Gleaming in the golden sunshine the pearl gray suburban station of Spanish mission design; sentinel palm trees rearing high aloft; a very smartly-dressed throng, several gentlemen arriving on horseback, handsome Airedales leaping on before, grooms following in the rear.

"What would you say," I asked, "was its source: this affinity, apparently, of San Francisco with ancient Greece? Greek theaters all about, Greek dances everywhere."

"Why, funny thing!" he answered. "I've just written an editorial about that. A similarity of climatic conditions, for one thing: opportunity here for open-air performances all the year round. Then this is, too, a seaport, and a city of much mingling of races."

* * * * * * *

Of course, I was continually asked if I had met George Sterling. "No, not yet." "But he lives over there at the Bohemian Club—you certainly must not miss seeing him!"

I did, however, by one accident and another, repeatedly miss him. Then it came about in this way that by chance I saw him: Proprietor of a book store, Mr. Newbegin, was to have the Mayor's secretary tour me about through places difficult of access to the stranger. But something prevented the attendance of the Mayor's secretary on the visitor so to have been honored; so that night we went instead, a party of us conveyed by Mr. Newbegin at a very exhilarating clip in his machine, to a very pleasant resort some distance out on the beach, where later on much charm was contributed to the dance by the arrival of a bevy of Raymond Hitchcock's "Hitchy-Koo" lasses.

Then my new friend, Leon Gelber (young man in the book department at the White House) said that an excellent thing to do would be to have a talk with Pauline Jacobson, whose career as a newspaper woman had given her much lore of San Francisco. We found her at dinner in a restaurant in the Italian quarter—a thriving place much frequented by spirits of literary and artistic tendency. Miss Jacobson proposed that we borrow a detective from the police department to go around with us some night soon. She also very cordially invited us to the "first social and dance" shortly to be given by the Bernal Heights Athletic Club, an organization of youthful, amateur prize-fighters in a very hardy part of town; at which function Miss

Jacobson, as the principal patroness of the society, was to lead the dance with the local butcher.

While we talked I had been observing at a nearby table a figure of more than a little distinction in effect. I could not at first explain to myself why this countenance, which I knew to be that of a stranger to me, should have a character so familiar. Then as the long, aristocratic, delicately carven features, under a tumbled shock of graying hair, were turned from profile directly toward me, I recognized the resemblance. It was a face strikingly like that handsome poet's mask of Richard Le Gallienne. "Yes," said Pauline, "that is George Sterling now."

(Perhaps I should explain that Miss Jacobson, as George Douglas puts it, "belongs," and so it is customary for her friends to refer to her as Pauline.) As with his party (two young women) he passed our table she called to him. He paused a moment. Not quite so tall as Mr. Le Gallienne, slighter in build. Very modest in manner, gentle of speech. Expression thoughtful, countenance (I felt) somewhat worn. Though we again arranged for a meeting, this (I cannot recall why) fell through, too; and I did not see him again.

* * * * * * *

"But, you know," said Pauline, "until four years ago we never had any paper money at all out here, nothing but gold and silver."

As those of us accustomed to "currency" all do, I was speaking of their silver "cartwheels" —and how I found it necessary to keep one suspender jacked up much firmer than the other, and then went about feeling that I walked like a postman, weighted down on one side.

"Well, when I was in the East," she replied, "I couldn't stand it—those bills always given me; had them changed for silver, so that I could feel I had some money."

* * * * * * *

A night or two later, past that quaint little Park, Portsmouth Square, where prosperous Chinatown merges into the Italian quarter, and where in the center of the park the graceful little ship rides on its tall pedestal graved "To Remember Robert Louis Stevenson"—past Portsmouth Square and then a short step downhill to the right to a police station there, where we picked up the detective assigned to be loaned to us. With our cicerone through strange ways: into shy courts and twisting alleys; up narrow, winding, murky stairways; along intricate corridors; through secret, panel doors (sometimes marked by the batterings of former police raids), with bolts upon bolts, chains and oaken bars at their back; down difficult ladders into pits of ebony blackness; then down more ladders, and still more—in short, here and there in that amazing labyrinth, now deserted, which was one time, not so long ago, a subterranean city of gambling and opium solace.

* * * * * * *

"And where do you go next?" they asked, everybody asked. Spirit of happiness in the air. Smiling approval of my doings. "Why, I'm going to Los Angeles very shortly," I would reply. Sudden dismay. Pall would fall upon the company. Ominous shaking of heads. "You won't like it there," the general conviction. Why not? "Bad climate; hot, sticky. Nothing there but 'one-lungers' and the movies"—and so on. Over and over repeated in San Francisco, this scene. Almost had me scared out of going to Los Angeles, this universal sentiment. "Certainly these people know more about the matter than I do," I said to myself. "Doubtless I'll not like the place. Why not stay here. I don't *have* to go there."

At the first of the following week I had planned to go. (This was the middle of the week.) I was walking along Market Street about ten in the morning. I was not thinking about Los Angeles. I was not thinking about San Francisco. I cannot recall that I was definitely thinking of anything. Well, probably, I was simply enjoying the exhilaration of my movement through an animated scene. Suddenly I had one of those mysterious calls of the spirit: I would go to Los Angeles, at once. Rapidly to the Ferry House. "Tell me a good train to-day to Los Angeles." "At five this afternoon," he said.

That is the way I transact business.

CHAPTER XVII

I BECOME A MOVIE "DIRECTOR"

I HAVE an aunt there. She (I had wired) met me at the train. By nine in the morning I was installed at the Alexandria. I went forth to look at the city. I liked it, its physiognomy, immensely. In my heart a lark was singing. At Fifth and Hill Streets I went into the delightful little park where so many pigeons stroll about the walks. Then I had some "California orange juice" at one of those innumerable, immaculate little stands. Next I was shaved. I began to feel a fury at the barber—would he never, never, never be done!

I was turning back the way I had come. I was not (this time) conscious of anything seriously wrong with me. Suddenly—Bang!—something seemed to have hit me a terrific blow! But the smash had come, apparently, not from without, but, curiously enough, from within my body. I began to tremble and shake, to find

[245]

enough breath only with great difficulty, and to feel that at any moment I might pitch headlong upon the pavement.

So! another one of my celebrated death scenes, first staged in Indianapolis. Would I be able to make my hotel? Heaven alone knew! I sought to measure with my eye the distance to be traveled. And I saw coming down the middle of the street . . . I cannot say that I almost fainted with astonishment at what I saw, as I was very nearly in a faint already. Rather, I think my amazement at the apparition before me revived me for a moment. Approaching me (coming for me, as it seemed) was a street-car labeled, "Crown Hill."

"In the name of all that's holy!" I cried, "if that damn'd car hasn't followed me two thousand miles!"

(I learned later that the Los Angeles Crown Hill is a recreation Park, not, like the Indianapolis Crown Hill, a cemetery.)

* * * * * * *

I wish to announce here a remarkable medical discovery. We are all acquainted with the idea of the beneficent effect on a patient of a physician's personality, his manner. Often more potent, perhaps, than his drugs. But little attention, I fear, has been paid to the therapeutic significance of a physician's dress. I was much heartened in the afternoon by the amiable and magnetic presence of Dr. George L. Cole, and much calmed by his prescriptions; but it was that evening when he turned up in his dinner jacket that I arose from my bed inspired to join (albeit with something of a totter) in the zest of life.

I most heartily recommend what I discovered by repetition to be his sartorial practice to the medical fraternity, particularly in the cases of life or death.

* * * * * * *

Maybe you will recall that at the time of your first visit to California you were a matter of astonishment to the people there. . . . "What! Never been here before!" Incredible, certainly.

Well, despite the fact that I had neglected them so long, everybody I met seemed glad to see me. Brightly: "and by what way did you come to Los Angeles?" I had, I said, been for several weeks in San Francisco. "Oh!" the reply; sad faces then all round. What was the matter with San Francisco? Well, I learned that it was a terrible place: awful climate, high winds, cold, fogs, no home life there, apartments, hotels, and so on much more.

* * * * * * *

I had wondered when first I arrived in Los Angeles what in special it would be that was going on that day. Never had I seen on ordinary occasions such throngs on the sidewalks of any city, every one in holiday attire, or what in its jubilant colors anywhere else certainly would have the effect of particularly festive holiday attire. The scene, however, was merely the way Los Angeles "goes on" all the time. "Looks like Indianapolis on Saturday nights when the When band used to play," said a cousin of mine I discovered practicing medicine in the city. Happy, humorous parallel, and quaint memory! . . . On Saturday nights when the When band used to play and all Indianapolis "dressed up" and came "down town" to promenade.

Or an amusing conceit rather, not an apt parallel. Indianapolis, of course, was never anything like this. Nor is New York.

"Now to Detroit, let us say," spoke my cousin, "you may have gone, or you may go, or you may not. Los Angeles is like New York in that everybody turns up there now and then, or sometime."

"But it's a different picture," I said; "a picture in a much gayer color scheme, done, so to say, with a much lighter touch, and with more verve and go." And I remembered what some one had told me: "That's not America out there. You'll find it is a foreign country."

Can you get on a train at Erewhon Junction rather plain as to face and figure and get off at Los Angeles a beautiful woman? The mystery of the thing, why every type and age of woman here should be so beautiful, continued to bother me. "Well, I don't know," said my doctor cousin, "a good many of them come to see me. They all want to be more slim, or more plump, or something else—all want, in some way, to be more beautiful."

* * * * * * *

Doubtless I am a highly irritable man. I got into a squabble with the hotel telephone operator. As I was about to hang up the receiver in my room, after reproving her the second time, I overheard her remark, aside, to some one in the office below: "Well, I thought that boy had left home!" Rather witty, I thought.

* * * * * * *

MEN AND BOOKS AND CITIES

At breakfast in an excellent little restaurant I was reading a copy of the magazine section of the Los Angeles *Times,* which I found in a pile of papers there. I was particularly interested in an "announcement" (running to something like a page and a half) of the "recent removal of the world's literary capitol to Los Angeles." Three classes of authors were presented as being here at present: one group writing short stories and novels; another writing stories to be "picturized"; a third group here to supervise the "picturization" of their stories and plays which had already met with popular success when published or acted. Among others (I've probably missed a number) named as present part or all the year were:—Rupert Hughes, Gertrude Atherton, Mary Roberts Rinehart, Rex Beach, Peter B. Kyne, Gouverneur Morris, Cosmo Hamilton, Harold McGrath, Wallace Irwin, Will Levington Comfort, Ellis Parker Butler, Winchell Smith, Walt Mason, William Allen White, Wallace Rice, Francis Grieson, Eugene Manlove Rhodes, Frank Condon, Elmer Harris, Bayard Veiller, Octavus Roy Cohan, Thompson Buchanan, Basil King, LeRoy Scott, and John Burroughs.

I BECOME A MOVIE "DIRECTOR"

Then I went into one of those numerous bright and cheery "pressing parlors," to see what they were like. I don't know whether or not you have been in any of them. Well, the window says you can be pressed in eight minutes (not long ago it had taken me two days to get back a suit from a hotel "valet"). You see at the back of the shop a row of little compartments (something like telephone booths) labeled "Dressing Rooms." When the door of one of these is open that means it is available. You enter, dump everything out of your pockets onto a little table, press a bell, door opens the width of a crack; you hand your suit to a hand thrust through, sit down and read a copy of *The Saturday Evening Post*—never any literature in these places except that journal. Within four minutes a hand thrusts in to you your trousers and waistcoat. You put these on, turn about, and the hand presents you with your coat. You come out two minutes to the good, pressed as fashionably as anything.

You go down the street; and (if you have the fresh eye of the stranger) you are struck by the extraordinary number of stationery stores, each of remarkable size—it would seem, indeed, that an army of writers inhabits Los Angeles. You are struck by the number of "art" shops. By the number of fine "markets." By the extraordinary number of places where magazines are displayed in profusion for sale. By the remarkably handsome bank buildings. By (if it is meal time) the long queues before the numerous "cafeterias." By (if it is evening) the long, long queues before the picture theaters. By the frequency of "taxidermy studios." By (if it be the beginning or the close of a week-end) the streams of young women "hikers," in their jolly, picturesque "knickers." By the beauty of the mountains at the end of the street. But, most of all, you are struck by the amazing number of photographers' establishments; by the very high excellence, in general, of the work they display, by (of course) the invariable beauty of the women who have been before their cameras, —and by the vast number of their productions which exhibit feminine loveliness in some degree of nudity, in subjects ranging from "California bathing girls" to poses in some form of "Greek classical dance."

These are some of the things which strike the mind of the innocent observer. As I was going along that day, I was struck in the chest, a whack of greeting by the friendly fist of my old friend, Alfred Kreymborg—benedict now, published poet, acted playwright, paid lecturer, accomplished mustache-wearer and cane-carrier, whom I used to know as a denizen of Fourteenth Street, about fifteen years ago, before he was any of these things.

* * * * * * *

I was on my way to see a bookseller celebrated (in the trade) nationally, C. C. Parker. Slender, alert, gray, pleasantly cosmopolitan in mind and manner; a gentleman whose idea of a friendly reception to a stranger is to loan him half the Parker stock to read, guard his health, cash his checks, and board him at the cozy Los Angeles Club, which overlooks the little park I have mentioned.

Besides Mr. Parker's extensive place, there are a couple of other good book stores in Los Angeles, Fowler Brothers and the Jones Book Store; also two or three first-rate department stores carry very fair stocks of books, notably one called Bullocks. Then, in addition, there are a surprising number of second-hand book stores, of a curious character. They have no front walls to them; but are open to the street all the way across from side to side. They do not close on Sundays; whether there is any manner of closing them up at all or not, I'm sure I don't know.

A matter for THE BOOKMAN to note, too, is that out this way you are likely to find (what you do not always find in some cities of considerable size in the Middle West) the leading newspapers carrying regularly on Saturdays or Sundays a full page of book reviews and news. Not only that but the literary editors of these papers care not a rap for expense in the matter of entertaining visitors in the literary business. They relish hugely blowing out three tires in an afternoon showing you the environs of their city. I have here in mind particularly a very entertaining afternoon spent with Thomas F. Ford (author of a recently published book, "The Foreign Trade of the United States"), Sunday Magazine editor of the Los Angeles *Times,* and who with his wife, Lillian C. Ford, gets up the book page of that paper. A member of the party was a gentleman now resident here who is closely affiliated with Eastern journalism, W. J. Ghent, a contributor to *The Nation* and *The New Republic.*

* * * * * * *

I paused on Broadway—I like the effect of the principal street of a city being named Broadway; you usually find in your travels some disreputable back alley called Fifth Avenue, or some horrible dump of a lodging-house named the Waldorf. I paused on Broadway to read a sign. It said:

> Why Pay Rent?
>
> Buy a furnished
>
> Summer Home on
>
> Wheels. And go
>
> Where you please.
>
> Ready for the Road
>
> In Five minutes.

* * * * * * *

I have not been exactly what you could call "addicted" to the movies. I do not say it as a boast; but to explain that I was ill acquainted

[255]

with them. When I wrote back to New York that I had got the movie habit, my correspondent replied: "Do you know, Murray, what you said the last time I asked you to take me to the movies? You replied: 'I'll gladly die for you; but I won't go with you to the movies.'"

In fact, the last time I did go to a motion-picture show (before I came out here) the circumstances were as follows: This was perhaps a couple of years ago. In a club I was set upon by my friend Reginald Birch, who declared that it was necessary for him to go to a movie show that night—as he would have to be shaved in the morning—that he couldn't go alone; and that I should have to go with him. The facts, it appeared, were these: His barber had a baby who was being shown on the screen at a certain picture theater; Mr. Birch, yielding to the father's natural pride, had declared that he would go to see this wonderful spectacle; and he could not again face his barber until he could say that he had done this. It was a terrible show; one of those two-cast-away-on-a-desert-island affairs. We sat, in an endeavor to avoid the pain of following the story, attempting to keep our minds in as much of a torpor as possible. The baby did not appear until the very end. The instant it was flashed upon the screen we grabbed our hats, fled to a cab, and drove rapidly away.

But, as I say, my experience of the pictures had been meager and unfortunate.

* * * * * * *

I have been told that many persons have said that after seeing the various processes in the production of a film the "romance" of the movies had been "spoiled" for them. I found the matter precisely the other way. I saw into only the better "studios," and but a couple of those. All in all, I was very favorably impressed indeed by what appeared to me to be evidence of a concrete endeavor, and a zest in striving to lift the art and the science of motion picture production continually to a higher plane.

To Culver City first I went. Being unacquainted with the technic of being admitted to such handsomely enclosed places of this nature, I first attempted to walk in at an entrance marked, "This gate for extra talent only." Having found the right door, I waited in a little office for the acquaintance I had made the other night, Thomas N. Miranda, whose official title, I believe, is that of "editor" for this "corporation."

Here I was struck by the superior character of the single decoration of this office—a more un-motion-picture-like thing would be hard to imagine. Indeed, the thought came to me that the dignity of the effect was startlingly unlike the office of any first-rate book publishing house I know; where you generally see something like the originals of Harrison Fisher illustrations framed on the walls. Above the landing at a turn of the stairs before me hung a huge canvas: a team of oxen mounting a swell of half-tilled ground; the admirable painting of the thing suggesting the influence of the school of Theodore Rousseau. Near me on the bench where I sat was another waiting: a very much "dolled up" child, who was what some might call a "fierce blood."

Out on the "lot" I walked across a public square in Petrograd, which by a few alterations had been converted from somewhere in Berlin; through a street of New York's East-side, which had formerly done duty as a scene in White-chapel, and later on would be something else again; along the main highway of Charlestown in 1860, which was but a few feet from a handsome view of Constantinople (all these things without any backs to them), and so on.

A new wrinkle in the matter of "shooting" the "sets" greatly took my fancy. This is the practice (now, I believe, introduced generally) of having music played while the actors perform before the camera. The effect is most entertaining, I think, in the small sets on the "dark stage" —that is the little domestic scenes taken indoors. I remember one in particular with much entertainment: A figure got up to look like a gentleman—dressing-gown, spats, monocle—is seated by a little table on which is his morning's mail.

Somebody cries: "All set?" Somebody sings out in reply: "All set!" Somebody barks: "Shoot!" The orchestra strikes up; the gentleman flourishes an ivory paper-cutter—and you have never seen such spirited mail-opening in your life. In comes some sort of an attendant. The gentleman looks up at him, and (simulating vivacious speech) works his jaws at him to the tune of the music. The attendant (to the tune of the music) grins down at the gentleman in reply; then sprays his mouth, with much liveliness. Suddenly music stops—all over—and the life seems to go out of the world.

[259]

Of a very interesting thing I heard: an interior representing St. Patrick's Cathedral was required. So they built an interior of the cathedral, at least an interior of one corner of it, sculpture and all. Prominent in the scene a very large figure of Christ—or rather, half a figure of Christ; the side away from the camera being open and exposing the lathe and plaster construction within. Coming by chance one day at lunch hour into this "cathedral," Mr. Miranda saw a workman on his knees, head bowed, before the gigantic figure. It was a carpenter praying before the half of an effigy he had helped to build.

To the lunch room on the lot, common to all; where fifteen thousand a year sits down with fifteen a week. And where (each in his or her make-up) the *Grande Dame,* with powdered hair, sits *tête-à-tête* with the old bum in tatters. Here I ran into Clayton Hamilton, looking more subdued than I had ever seen him before. He had but very recently arrived, and was docilely submitting himself (as he put it, in the "primary class") to instruction in the "picture game."

Back with Miranda to his office. A slot is cut in the face of his work-table, through which gleams a bright light below. The film, wound on reels at either side, is made to pass over this slot for his minute inspection—for his "editing," that is; which is the process of rearranging the order of scenes to a more effective presentation of the story; or of "cutting" so many feet, and then "joining up" smoothly the severed parts.

Was telling me, Tom, with much gusto, of an amusing "Edgar" story by Tarkington now being filmed. Little darky plays Hamlet. To the question, "Who's you?" he replies, "I's yo' pappie's ghost." "When," I asked, "did you get the 'script' of this?" "About two months ago," he said. Well, I declare! And so that's how Tarkington came to have that great "Hamlet" bug at just about that time when I saw him in Indianapolis! "Why don't the Prince kill the King," and so on. Was working on this nigger version of the play.

In San Francisco I had the honor one time of being mistaken for a "cattleman." At Culver City I met, on one occasion, with even greater esteem. It was in one of the "dark rooms" where the films wound on tall frames are "dipped" into long, narrow vats of developing liquid. A very feeble red light had been turned on for my benefit. I heard a voice in my ear:

"Didn't I see you the other night at the Alexandria?" I turned and made out in the faint glow a horribly besmirched boy garbed in a weirdly-stained undershirt. "Probably," I replied; "I'm stopping there." "Oh! I know," he said; "you are a director."

That night in the lobby of the hotel I was listening to the conversation around me: "Well, I don't know, they 'cut' more stuff in New York"; and so on. I became conscious that a very, an exceedingly fashionable-looking youth seated on a divan not far away was eyeing me. Against each of his arms reclined a very dashing-looking miss, a very modish-looking miss, indeed. He disengaged himself, came over to me and introduced himself. "Don't you remember? I met you out on the lot to-day," he said. He was a generous, an open-handed youth. He offered to divide his ladies with me. "Let's go somewhere, the four of us," he said, "and jazz." I declined, abashed; I did not feel myself sufficiently smart for such society.

*   *   *   *   *   *   *

Then the goodly Odysseus of the hardy heart turned his face toward Ithaca—home.

*   *   *   *   *   *   *

I BECOME A MOVIE "DIRECTOR"

As I was checking out of the hotel I caught a letter, from one Marjorie. It began:

You're writing a new book, I hear. "Men and Books and Cities," or something of the sort. It sounds unreal, reflections of reflections of reality. Just the sort of thing every one's expecting you to write. Good stuff, I doubt not. But I had you down for something really creative this time, an attempt to thrust through to life itself.

Quite so! Quite so!
The letter continued:

I often wonder about you and how you are getting on. And where it will all end for you. I've made up several ends for you; but somehow they aren't true—aren't inherent in the case as true things must be.

My "end"? I'm sure I haven't the least idea about it. Meanwhile there is

"Laughter and the love of friends."